Leaving Care

Leaving Care

Throughcare and Aftercare in Scotland

Jo Dixon and Mike Stein

Jessica Kingsley Publishers
London and Philadelphia

First published in 2005
by Jessica Kingsley Publishers
116 Pentonville Road
London N1 9JB, UK
and
400 Market Street, Suite 400
Philadelphia, PA 19106, USA

www.jkp.com

Library of Congress Cataloging in Publication Data
Dixon, Jo, 1967-
 Leaving care : throughcare and aftercare in Scotland / Jo Dixon and Mike Stein.
  p. cm.
 Includes bibliographical references and index.
 ISBN-13: 978-1-84310-202-1 (pbk. : alk. paper)
  ISBN-10: 1-84310-202-1 (pbk. : alk. paper) 1. Youth—Services for—Scotland. 2.
Youth—Institutional care—Scotland. 3. Youth—Deinstitutionalization—Scotland. 4. Social
work with youth—Scotland. I. Stein, Mike. II. Title.

 HV1441.G8S35 2005
 362.7'09411—dc22

                                                                                2005018119

British Library Cataloguing in Publication Data
A CIP catalogue record for this book is available from the British Library

ISBN-13: 978 1 84310 202 1
ISBN-10: 1 84310 202 1

Printed and Bound in Great Britain by
Athenaeum Press, Gateshead, Tyne and Wear

Contents

Tables

Figures

Acknowledgements

We are grateful to the many people who have contributed to the completion of this book. First, our thanks to the local authorities and external agencies that took part in our research, in particular the managers, social workers and leaving care workers who, in addition to their own busy workload, were willing to spare some of their time to contribute to the study.

We would also like to thank Dr Rod Harrison and the members of our advisory groups both at the Scottish Executive and at Barnardo's Scotland, our partners in the research, as well as Alison Caulfield-Dow from the Scottish Throughcare and Aftercare Forum and representatives from Who Cares? Scotland, all of whom provided us with invaluable advice, information and support throughout the study.

Thanks to Jim Wade and Gwyther Rees for methodological and statistical guidance, to Dawn Rowley for preparing the manuscript and to Kimberly Foley, Ian Wood, Tam Baillie and Sandra Brown, Neil McMillan, Lesley Sloan, Scott Telfer, Gill Levy, Nicky Campbell and Froya Rossvoll for their important contributions to the study.

Finally, and most importantly, we would like to thank the young people who were willing to share their stories, experiences and insights with us. We hope we have done justice to their views.

Chapter 1

Introduction and Background

Introduction

'I'm only 16 and still a bairn and get a bit weepy at times.' (Heather)

For most young people their journey to adulthood is exciting and daunting. It is a time of choices, opportunities and risks, as they go on to college or work, make new friends, and move on from their family to set up home. For many young people today this journey extends into their mid-twenties, and most remain dependent on their families for financial, practical and personal support. But for those who leave care, often at just 16 or 17, life can be far more difficult. Coping with such major changes in their lives can be overwhelming, especially if they have problems from the past and lack support.

This book is about the experiences of young people leaving care in Scotland and the key developments in policy and practice aimed at supporting them during their journey to adulthood. It explores their experiences of care, leaving care and their lives after care as they move on to independent living. It also considers the role of support services, both in terms of the wider context in which they are organised and how they are working in practice to assist young people. Importantly, this book seeks to address the questions of how these two elements, their experiences and support interventions, might impact upon their future lives, and what messages can be carried forward to aid our understanding of what helps to promote positive life choices and chances for those in and leaving care.

The book draws and expands upon the findings of a two-year research study of throughcare (support to prepare young people for leaving care) and aftercare (support for young people who have moved on from care) services for young people leaving care under the Children (Scotland) Act 1995 (Dixon and Stein 2002a). In addition to the original material from the research, the book includes further outcome analysis and a discussion, in our concluding chapter, of updated policy developments carried out between 2002 and 2005.

This research study brings together information from a number of key sources, including policy and practice data collected from a national postal survey of all Scottish local authorities and a range of other agencies involved in the provision of throughcare and aftercare support. It also draws upon information gathered from young people and their leaving care support workers and from interviews carried out with senior social work managers and leaving care team leaders, as well as representatives of other services involved in supporting young people. Taken together, it considers the leaving care experience from the perspectives of a broad range of key players, and thereby provides a rounded insight into what it means to move on from care in Scotland and what works in promoting positive life chances for care-experienced young people in general.

The following sections look at how and why the research was conducted. We start by considering the wider context in which the research is situated.

Background to the research

The study was carried out against a background of existing research evidence and a broad range of legislative and policy and practice developments.

Previous research

Turning first to previous research, there have been a number of studies over the past three decades that have focused on the experience and outcomes for those who have been looked after in public care (see Stein 2004 for a summary of these studies). We will draw on these findings in greater detail throughout later chapters, but at this stage a general outline should set the scene.

Evidence from this previous research shows that care leavers are a diverse group in terms of their pre-care experiences, their reasons for entering care, their care histories, their needs and abilities, and their ethnic backgrounds. Some young people will have positive and valued experiences of being looked after while for others it may generate further problems. They may experience further disruption through placement movement, the erosion of family and community links and the failure to have their basic developmental, educational and health needs met.

In addition, a majority of young people leaving care will move to independent living at just 16 or 17 – whereas most young people remain at home well into their twenties – and for many of these young people, leaving care is final; the option to return in times of difficulty is rare. But not only do young people leave care for independent living earlier than their non-care peers, they have to cope with major changes in their lives – learning to manage a home, finding their way into education, training or employment, or coping with unemployment or starting a family – in the early period after leaving care. In short, many have accelerated and compressed transitions to adulthood.

In this context, it is not surprising that research studies, completed between the mid-1970s and mid-1990s, have provided evidence of the high risk of social exclusion for care leavers – especially through homelessness, loneliness, isolation, unemployment, poverty and mental health problems (see Biehal *et al.* 1995; Broad 1998, 1999; Stein and Carey 1986). Although much of this research was carried out in England, similar findings emerged from Scotland where a number of small-scale descriptive studies documented poor planning, preparation and aftercare support and the difficulties experienced by many young people leaving the care of Scottish local authorities (Emond 2000; Morgan-Klein 1985; Triseliotis *et al.* 1995).

Evidence from research, together with the growing concerns of those working with care leavers about poor outcomes and the lack of focused support, contributed to the introduction of specialist leaving care projects from the late 1980s onwards. The development of these projects took place across the different countries of the UK, including Scotland. Such projects, though variable in size and organisation, generally aimed to provide a more focused response to the core needs of care leavers, in particular for accommodation, personal support, finance and help with careers. An evaluation of four projects carried out in England provided evidence that they could contribute to positive outcomes for care leavers, especially taking into account their very poor starting points (Biehal *et al.* 1995).

The legal context
With regards to the legislative context within which our research was situated, one of the most important developments was the Children (Scotland) Act 1995, which came into force in April 1997. This Act (and the accompanying Regulations and Guidance) included new duties and powers for local authorities in respect of 'throughcare': to provide advice and assistance with a view to preparing the child for when he or she is no longer looked after (S.17) and 'aftercare': to provide advice, guidance and assistance to young people who have left care up to the age of 19, and for some young people up to the age of 21 (S.29.1) (Scottish Office 1997). The Act

also stresses the importance of the corporate responsibilities of local authorities, as well as the need to work with other agencies; both are crucial to providing effective arrangements for care leavers.

In addition to the Children (Scotland) Act 1995, a number of policy developments and initiatives carrying important implications for young people looked after in and leaving care were introduced during the course of our research. These included new funding sources for care leavers and for young people with drug problems (the Children's Services Development Fund and the Changing Children's Services Fund); improved housing plus support (through the transitional arrangements for Supporting People) and funding opportunities to assist young people leaving care with post-16 education, employment and training (through proposals outlined in the Beattie Report).

The most significant of these further developments was the Children (Leaving Care) Act 2000 introduced in England and Wales in October 2001 (Broad 2005). Its provisions included the transfer of financial support for 16- and 17-year-olds from the Department for Work and Pensions (DWP) to local authorities throughout the UK. However, its implementation was delayed in Scotland to await the recommendations of the Working Group on Throughcare and Aftercare set up by the Scottish Executive. This group was to consider both the timing of the financial transfer and how local authorities might improve current services in the context of the Act. We explore these developments further in the concluding chapter of the book.

Within this overall context of the research and legislative background, statutory and voluntary groups working with young people leaving care in Scotland wanted to know how young people were being prepared and supported after care by leaving care services. The absence of any large scale, empirical Scottish research led to the commissioning, by the Scottish Executive, of this research: the first national study of leaving care in Scotland.

How was the research conducted?

From our own point of view, as researchers, we are often inclined towards an equal interest in the *process* as well as the *outcomes* of an undertaking. With that in mind, and in seeing this book as an outcome of our research, we feel that it is important to be clear about the process, or methods, by which the research study was carried out. However, not all readers will share this interest, so for the sake of brevity we have limited this section to a basic overview of the key points necessary for understanding how the information contained within this book was gathered and used. For those readers who are interested in finding out more about the processes by which the study was conducted, for example, the key questions and aims underpinning the research, the sampling criteria and how the data was collected and analysed, a detailed methodology has been provided in Appendix A.

Design of the research

The research study on which this book is based was carried out between 1999 and 2001. In short, the study provided an exploration of how support for young people leaving care works in practice within the wider policy context of throughcare and aftercare under the Children (Scotland) Act 1995.

The study comprised two stages. The first involved a national policy survey of Scottish local authorities (31 out of 32 authorities, 97%, responded to our questionnaire) and a survey of other relevant service providers (99 out of 178, 56%, questionnaires were returned).[1]

The second stage involved case studies of three local authorities, selected to be representative of the main models of leaving care service and the geographic diversity of Scotland. This stage involved a survey of 107 young people and their main support workers (77% of support workers responded). A sub-sample of these young people (n=61) also took part in a six-month follow-up study. Follow-up information was also provided by 58 per cent of support workers.

Data collection and analysis

Data was collected via postal questionnaires, face-to-face interviews, telephone interviews and reviews of policy and practice documents.

Our main approach to analysing the data was quantitative and involved the use of statistical tests using the statistical package for the social sciences (SPSS). For ease of reading we have tried to keep our reporting of statistical tests to a minimum throughout the book. In most cases we will simply give the p-value if a test was statistically significant.[2] Test results and p-values have been reported as a way of supporting our findings. For those readers who prefer to do so, however, it is possible to ignore references to the statistical results throughout the book without losing any of the key information or meaning of the text.

Qualitative data has been used to provide case illustrations and a descriptive account of the processes and experiences of leaving care from the perspective of young people and their workers.

Outline of the book

The structure of the book has been organised so as to lead the reader through the care, leaving care and aftercare experiences of the young people who took part in the study. Information on the policy and practice context has largely been incorporated into relevant chapters, and will be brought together with the key findings in the Conclusion.

This first chapter presents the research and policy background against which our study of leaving care was set. It also describes the study in terms of its main aims and the methods employed to gather and analyse the data.

Chapter 2 outlines the two models of leaving care services that we found in our policy survey, a non-specialist service and a centrally organised specialist scheme. We also describe the three very different local authorities that were selected to be representative of these models, as well as the geographical and socio-economic diversity of Scotland.

In Chapter 3 we introduce the young people who participated in our study and describe their care histories and their experiences of education, as well as what they considered to be the 'good' and 'bad' things about their lives in care.

Chapter 4 explores the process of preparation, first of all from the findings of our policy survey, and then from the perspective of young people and their support workers.

In Chapter 5 we describe young people's experiences of moving on from the care of our three local authorities. This includes an exploration of the process of leaving, as well as an account of their initial destinations and outcomes.

How were our young people supported after they left care? In Chapter 6, having set the context through the findings of our policy survey, we look at the different sources of support, formal and informal, that our young people received when they were trying to establish independent lives.

At this time of their lives, young people's needs are often met by different agencies. Chapter 7 presents the findings from our policy survey of how the different agencies saw their involvement with young people. It then describes how young people viewed the support they received.

What made a difference to the lives of the young people who participated in our study? In Chapter 8 we identify and discuss what contributed to the likelihood of successful and unsuccessful transitions and outcomes for young people leaving care. This key chapter focuses on young people who took part in the six-month follow-up study and brings together their experiences, the preparation and aftercare support they received and their outcomes across a range of life areas after leaving care.

In our concluding chapter we reflect upon the main findings from our study and explore the implications for the development of throughcare and aftercare services.

Notes

1   In all, 178 other agencies were contacted. This included local authority housing departments and education departments, employment services, the Scottish Children's Reporters Administration and a range of other agencies, such as health boards, primary care trusts, other housing providers and a range of specialist and voluntary projects offering support to young people.

2   A result of $p=0.05$ or less was considered statistically significant for our data. This may be reported as $p=$ followed by the value. Occasionally we have reported the test as $p<$ which simply means p is less than. By way of a brief explanation, a p-value gives the probability that a test result can be relied upon to be true, that is to say that it did not occur by chance. $P=0.05$ simply means that the probability of the result happening by chance is 5 in 100. $P<0.01$ means that the probability of a result happening by chance is less than 1 in 100, and so on. We have adopted the principle that a test result with a p-value of 0.05 or less is significant; that is to say that the result is unlikely to have happened by chance and is therefore likely to be true of the wider population.

Chapter 2

Throughcare and Aftercare Services in Three Authorities

Introduction

In this chapter we begin by outlining the findings from our policy survey of the main models of leaving care services that led to the selection of our three representative local authorities. We then describe each of the participating areas – County, City and Shire[1] – drawing upon different sources: demographic data, the policy information collected during our survey, and finally the policy interviews carried out with senior staff responsible for the provision of leaving care services in each of the selected areas.

Models of service delivery

Before beginning our study we identified three different authority-wide models of service provision derived from our earlier research work carried out in England (Biehal *et al.* 1995):

1. *A non-specialist service*: in this model responsibility for delivering a leaving care service rests primarily with field social workers or general childcare teams, sometimes in collaboration with other carers, particularly foster or residential carers.

2. *A centrally organised specialist scheme*: in this model services are provided by a centrally located team of specialist leaving care workers who provide an authority-wide service.

3. *A dispersed specialist scheme*: in this model individual specialist leaving care workers are attached to area-based fieldwork or childcare teams.

In addition, a survey of best practice in England carried out during 1999 identified a fourth model, *a centrally organised integrated service*, providing an integrated service to a wider range of vulnerable young people, including care leavers and other young people 'in need': for example, homeless young people, young offenders and young people who run away from home or care (Stein and Wade 2000).

Non-specialist service

Just under a third (32%) of social work departments had no specialist team or specialist staff with direct responsibility for providing throughcare and aftercare services. Most of these departments indicated that field social workers, residential social workers and foster carers were involved in providing these services. Most respondents, however, were unable to state the numbers of staff formally involved in providing a throughcare and aftercare service. Less than half (40%) had a written description of the range of throughcare and aftercare services provided.

Non-specialist services were generally being provided in larger rural areas, or in geographical areas where either the numbers of young people currently eligible to receive formal throughcare and aftercare or those who had been in receipt of throughcare and aftercare services in the past 12 months were lower.

Centrally organised specialist scheme

Our Scottish policy survey revealed that just over two-thirds of authorities (68%) had a specialist team or specialist staff with direct responsibility for providing throughcare and aftercare services. The numbers of specialist staff involved ranged in number from 1.5 to 40.5 reflecting in part the numbers of young people in receipt of throughcare and aftercare services within the local authorities. Over half (57%) of those who had a specialist team or specialist staff were centrally located, 71 per cent were managed by the social work department and 76 per cent were funded by the social work department. Funding exclusively by these departments ranged from £26,000 to £610,000 depending on the number of specialist staff employed.

The remaining specialist schemes included those jointly managed and funded by social work departments and the voluntary sector or other external agencies. All were centrally located. One social work department had two specialist teams located within different localities. Joint funding arrangements varied from equal matched funding between social work departments and voluntary or external agencies to 93 per cent social work department funding. Just over half (52%) of the specialist teams or specialist staff provided a service to all eligible young people within their authorities.

One provided services to all eligible groups except young people under the age of 16 who were looked after at home. The others provided aftercare services for young people not able to live at or return home. Over half (52%) of the specialist schemes reported having a written description of the services provided by the throughcare and aftercare team. This picture points to the centrally organised specialist scheme as the main specialist model. There was no evidence of dispersed specialist staff within fieldwork teams, although several respondents commented upon the links between their specialist teams and other carers. As detailed above, the main variation in the model was in respect of joint funding and managerial arrangements with the voluntary sector.

Selection of the case study authorities

On the basis of this response ratio (2:1), it was decided to select two areas (County and City) with a specialist leaving care service and one (Shire) with a non-specialist service. In addition, the areas were chosen to be representative of Scotland's geographical and socio-economic diversity.

County

Background

County has a total population of 349,200 people with 99.2 per cent of the population classified as White, 0.25 per cent Pakistani, 0.1 per cent Black, 0.1 per cent Indian, and 0.2 per cent as Other. Just under a quarter of the population are aged 18 or under. Southern and western County are predominantly large urban areas with an industrial economy – a mix of traditional industries, electronics and precision engineering combined with a large service sector – while the east is mainly agricultural and has a small tourist industry.

The overall unemployment rate is just under 9 per cent. However, the heritage of the industrial past has left significant areas of high unemployment and social deprivation. Nearly 25 per cent of school-age children live in families receiving financial support to provide school clothes, and 16.5 per cent of school-age children live in households dependent on income support or Jobseeker's Allowance. A further 12.5 per cent of children are in families in receipt of Family Credit or Disability Working Allowance. In County as a whole, the rate for looked after children is 5.4 per 1000 compared to a Scottish average of 10 per 1000.

Throughcare and aftercare services

ORGANISATIONAL FRAMEWORK AND APPROACH

County has a centrally organised specialist model. The project was set up in 1995 as a planned response to the new throughcare and aftercare provisions contained within the then Children (Scotland) Bill. It is a specialist service within the council's social work department. During the period of the research the project employed a team manager, three social workers and two part-time home carers, and covered the whole of the area. At the time of the policy survey (April 2000) the project's staffing costs were £114,000. More recent data gathered at the time of the policy interviews (September 2001) showed the overall budget for April 2000 to March 2001 to be £174,607, and estimated unit costs per young person per year at £1559. This excludes costs associated with a careers project (see below).

The main approach is to offer a specialist service to young people aged 15½ to 21 years who are in care or who have left care to live independently. For young people who live at home and who are eligible for services, these were agreed in advance, and will be provided by the local children and families team.

In January 2000 a careers project started and has, in effect, become another arm of the same service. It is managed by the throughcare team manager and works with excluded young people who face multiple barriers in accessing the local labour market, or in making sustainable progress towards education, employment or training. It targets young people in the process of leaving care, those in receipt of aftercare and young people living away from home in supported accommodation. It employs a careers advisor, a senior youth worker and two employability advisors.

The dedicated leaving care project and careers project are seen as offering an integrated and specialist approach. This work is set in a wider policy framework of corporate parenting – recognising the responsibility of all council departments to young people who are looked after in and leaving the public care system.

ELIGIBILITY FOR THROUGHCARE AND AFTERCARE

In the 12-month period up to May 2000 (questionnaire completion date), 111 young people received throughcare and aftercare services from the project. Thirty-five young people were in receipt of throughcare services and 76 young people were in receipt of aftercare services.

POLICY AND PROCEDURAL FRAMEWORK

There is a designated lead officer responsible for throughcare and aftercare services. The arrangements for providing throughcare and aftercare are contained within the Children's Services Plan[2] and there are authority-wide policies and procedures. Guidance is provided for social workers. A specially compiled care leavers' guide is distributed to young people.

THROUGHCARE

Preparing young people for leaving care is based on meeting each individual's needs as distinct from the provision of a formal programme approach targeted at children's homes or foster care. Identifying throughcare needs is carried out as part of the care planning and review process when young people reach 15 years of age: the work required, the workers responsible, and the target dates for tasks are documented at the outset in an Initial Action Plan. Ongoing work is recorded in the Review Action Plan. The *Looking After Children* materials (Department of Health 1995) are not currently in use in County.[3] Young people are involved in the whole process, by participating in the preparation of the care plan, attending reviews and completing their own reports, and in the construction of the Initial Action Plans.

AFTERCARE

Personal support

Eligible young people are referred to the project usually through the care planning process detailed above. In addition the project also considers referrals from other agencies and young people can self-refer. Young people are then allocated a specialist key worker who will be responsible for offering personal support and guidance in relation to a range of areas: accommodation, finance, practical living skills, emotional support and anything else in which the young person seeks assistance.

Accommodation

As part of its corporate parenting strategy, the social work department works collaboratively with the housing department. Young people leaving care are recognised as a priority group for housing needs assessment and two homelessness officers from County's council housing service act as link workers for the leaving care project. Also, there is a supported lodgings scheme, currently offering 21 places to young people aged 16 to 21 who leave care to live independently. Landlords and landladies offer home comforts as well as some additional support. Other available accommodation options include a supported hostel, semi-independent flats and council tenancies.

Financial assistance

Financial help includes: income 'top-up' payments, assistance with employment, further and higher education, accommodation subsidies, and meeting emergencies costs. During 2000 the project budget was £30,500 and the nine children and family teams held an additional £5850.

Education, employment and training

As part of the corporate parenting strategy, the careers project creates individual pathways for young people into education, employment and training. Following on from individual assessment young people are offered a wide-ranging programme that includes: one-to-one counselling; careers open drop-in sessions; focused group work sessions, covering confidence building, personal presentation, employability skills, job search skills, assertiveness skills and interview techniques; a young mothers' education initiative group; outdoor education courses and a young people's consultation group. An evaluation of the project (for the year 2000) based upon 55 young people showed that 64 per cent 'achieved desired progress'.

Health and personal development

In the main, advice on health and personal development is part of the key worker role. In addition, the project is involved in a specific initiative to improve sexual health by participating in the condom distribution scheme, whose primary goal is to prevent the spread of HIV. Also, it has been acknowledged that the mental health needs of young people (aged 15 to 25) in County need to be a greater priority and there are proposals to set up a multi-agency group to establish drop-in facilities for young people.

The model of service delivery in County is of a central specialist service, providing primary support to young people unable to return home, at the hub of intra-departmental throughcare and aftercare services, and wider inter-agency networks.

Monitoring and evaluation

County has developed an electronic database, which is used to collect and collate data on throughcare and aftercare services. By September 2001 this had been used to contribute to performance review information by providing essential data on throughcare and aftercare services. This included outcome data at two points in time: the time of discharge from care and the time when the case was closed. At both these times data was collected on age, areas of concern and vulnerability, occupation and accommodation, and, at Time 2 only, reasons for closure. County intends to develop the database further in order to collect more outcome data.

City
Background
City authority is Scotland's largest city with a population of 611,440, of whom 169,000 (27%) are children and young people under 21, and approximately 9,200 (5%) of these are from minority ethnic groups largely consisting of Pakistani, Indian, Chinese, Asian and Black groups.

City is an urban area and one of the UK's major manufacturing centres. Its industries include engineering, clothing, publishing and food and drink. City has the highest unemployment rate of any council in Scotland; male unemployment is 16.1 per cent and female 5.45 per cent, compared to a Scottish rate of 9.8 per cent and 3.3 per cent respectively. Almost 70 per cent of those unemployed are aged 20 to 24.

Poverty has a wide impact upon the lives of families, children and young people. The Scottish Office family stress indicator for City (derived from a combination of data on lone parents, unemployment, occupancy norms, large families and long-term illness) is the highest in Scotland at 221 (compared to a national average of 34). These levels of stress are also reflected in the numbers of young people looked after by local authorities in Scotland. City has 17 children per 1000 of the population looked after compared to a national average of 10 per 1000.

Throughcare and aftercare services
ORGANISATION AND APPROACH
City also has a centrally organised specialist model. Throughcare and after-care services are the responsibility of City Council's social work department. A specialist leaving care team is the organisational centre with responsibility for assessing all young people who are looked after and accommodated at 15 years of age. If the young person's care plan indicates that they are unable to return home the team will be responsible for primary support services. If the young person's care plan indicates an alternative plan, such as rehabilitation to the family home, then the specialist team will monitor this after six months and review future needs.

The team has a central office and employs 40.5 specialist staff. A careers advisor and two nurses are also based at the office. At the time of the policy survey (April 2000) the service cost just under £1m (£989,444), 93 per cent of which was funded by City Council and 7 per cent by external sources. No data on unit costs for throughcare and aftercare services was available.

In its primary support role the team is directly responsible for a group work programme, supported carers and supported tenancies. The team is also responsible for formal links with the department's nine area social work teams and residential services.

There are corporate links with City's housing department to provide emergency accommodation for care leavers. In terms of inter-agency links, the voluntary sector is also contracted to provide services through a Barnardo's 16+ project as well as a range of accommodation and residential care projects. The City's social work department is also partners with a Social Inclusion Partnership (SIP) working with young people leaving care in the city. The SIP aims, through partnership approaches, to improve services for young people leaving care. It is currently working on four fronts: research and information; education, training and employment; independent living; and health and well-being.

ELIGIBILITY FOR THROUGHCARE AND AFTERCARE

All young people who are looked after and accommodated in City – at home, in foster care and residential care (children's units, residential schools and secure accommodation) – are referred to the specialist leaving care team at age 15 to decide what throughcare and aftercare services they need. In April 2000 (policy questionnaire date), 301 young people were eligible for throughcare and 342 for aftercare. The number of young people leaving care aged over 16 was approximately 130 each year. As detailed above, the specialist leaving care team works mainly with young people who are not returning home. In April 2000, they were in contact with 330 young people and in April 2001 364 including both new and ongoing young people, aged 15 to 24.

POLICY AND PROCEDURAL FRAMEWORK

There is a designated lead officer for throughcare and aftercare services and the Children's Services Plan and annual review outline the arrangements for providing these services. Operational guidance and procedures are issued to staff and an explanatory leaflet is given to young people. Young people's views are actively sought by the department. They have been consulted on major reviews and policy developments including departmental policy (children's services); new funding bids (youth arts programme, mental health development fund); new activities (sports group) and service reviews (Best Value reviews, tenancies and carers' services).

THROUGHCARE

Young people aged 15 living in foster care or residential care and planning to move to independence are allocated a worker from the leaving care service who, in consultation with the young person, their family and relevant workers, prepares a throughcare assessment report. This identifies their preparation and support needs, including a plan for implementation, timescale and resourcing. The throughcare assessment is carried out using a specially compiled life skills pack. Identified needs are met through one-to-one work or group work. The *Looking After Children* action and assessment records (Department of Health 1995) are not currently being used.

AFTERCARE

Personal support

Young people receive personal support from a leaving care worker if they are moving to independence, or from an area team social worker if they are going home. In addition, the leaving care project provides a daily duty system for care leavers who are facing particular difficulties or emergencies: destitution, eviction, homelessness, addiction problems, emotional trauma and mental health emergencies. Also, personal support is provided by drop-in groups for care leavers and a weekly group specifically for care leavers with their own children. Both groups employ life skills and problem management approaches along with leisure and recreational features.

Accommodation

The leaving care services provide and purchase a range of supported accommodation. First, 48 supported carers provide a full-time family support setting for 34 to 40 young people and a respite, emergency resource for up to five young people. Second, 17 supported tenancies provide accommodation with external support for 23 young people. Finally, the service works in partnership with nine supported accommodation units and a range of voluntary organisations including Barnardo's 16+, to provide approximately 35 places for care leavers.

Financial assistance

Young people receive a £2500 start-up grant when moving to their own home and a further £500 for each child. In addition, discretionary assistance may be given to 'top up' income, meet accommodation costs, assist with employment or further and higher education, or meet any emergencies. The annual budget amounts to just under £2m – but this includes accommodation subsidies for all homeless young people.

Education, employment and training
The leaving care service provides specialist education, employment and training support for young people through a careers project which offers individual and group work support. In addition, social work services and City Building have collaborated in the development of a joint training programme for care leavers, which provides employment, training and apprenticeship opportunities.

Health and personal development
In addition to individual work undertaken that arises from the throughcare assessment, the leaving care service provides an emergency duty system. Also, during the course of the research a number of new initiatives were developed: six new drug worker posts were created to work with young people in care and care leavers to help them address their addictions; an initiative was set up to address health issues for young prostitutes; and a nursing service for care leavers was provided.

Monitoring and evaluation
During the period of the research an electronic database was set up to collect statistical information on throughcare and aftercare services. Data is collected on young people aged 15 to 24 who are in contact with the leaving care service. This includes data on placements, age and gender and accommodation after leaving care. There is no information collected in respect of young people leaving care who are not supported by either the area team social worker or residential social worker. However, City and the SIP are planning to set up a city-wide tracking system for all young people leaving care.

Shire
Background
Shire is a predominantly rural area in the north of Scotland with a population of 226,260. Ninety-nine per cent of the population is white and just over a quarter lives in the five main towns. Seven per cent of the population is pre-school age, 16 per cent school age, 62 per cent working age and 15 per cent retired. The population has a significantly higher proportion of

younger age groups than the rest of Scotland, reflecting recent employment-driven immigration.

Traditionally, Shire's economy has been dependent upon agriculture, fishing and forestry and related processing industries. However, since the mid-1970s, the emergence of the oil and gas industries and the development of tourism have broadened its economic base and led to rapid population growth. The service sector currently accounts for over half of employment (54%); manufacturing, construction, oil and gas 23 per cent; and the primary sector – agriculture, fishing and forestry – 5 per cent. Unemployment stands at 2.6 per cent, lower than either Scottish or UK rates. Shire also scores lowest on the Scottish Office family stress indicator (derived from a combination of data on lone parents, unemployment, occupancy norms, large families and long-term illness). Shire's rate for looked after children is 7 per 1000 compared to a Scottish average of 10 per 1000.

Throughcare and aftercare services

ORGANISATION AND APPROACH

Shire has had a joint housing and social work department since 1998. All childcare services, including throughcare and aftercare, are provided by children and family social work teams. These are located in the northern (one senior social worker and five social workers) and central and southern (one senior social worker and seven social workers) divisions of the county.

The main approach during the period of our research was a non-specialist hybrid model, social workers having responsibility for the range of childcare work within their caseloads. However, although this was the main approach, there were differences within the Shire. Whereas in central and southern divisions throughcare and aftercare was entirely non-specialist at the outset of the research, in the north, a Barnardo's 16+ team carried out aftercare. Also, during the course of the research, the southern division employed a half-time specialist aftercare worker and the central division appointed a full-time leaving care worker.

In this hybrid model, during the period of our research, all eligible young people from the central division and the majority from the southern division were receiving non-specialist services, while most of those from the north received specialist services provided by Barnardo's 16+ project. In all three divisions, the team social workers held case responsibility. There are two distinctive features of the approach. First, the development of individual tailor-made responses, especially through the use of the *Looking After Children* action and assessment records. Second, the commitment to involving young people both at an individual and a wider policy level.

ELIGIBILITY FOR THROUGHCARE AND AFTERCARE

Young people looked after at home, living in foster care, living in children's homes and those moving to independent living were eligible to receive throughcare while they were looked after, and aftercare services up to the age of 21.

However, during the period of the research there was no central collation of data for this age group – although this was planned for 2002 when the service was due to be reorganised. In response to the policy questionnaire, it was estimated that 105 young people had been in receipt of aftercare services in the 12-month period up to the end of May 2000 (including new and ongoing cases).

An independent consultant employed by the authority identified 217 young people aged 16 and over who ceased to be looked after since April 1996, comprising 101 young people leaving foster or residential care and 116 from being looked after at home. On this basis, and assuming equal year divisions (between April 1996 and May 2000) this would suggest 54 young people each year, 25 from foster or residential care and 29 from home, were eligible for aftercare services.

POLICY AND PROCEDURAL FRAMEWORK

Shire employs a lead officer with responsibility for throughcare and aftercare services. The arrangements for providing throughcare and aftercare are contained within the Children's Services Plan and written policy, procedures and practice material are provided separately in each of the three divisions. Guidance is made available to staff, foster and residential carers, young people and the voluntary sector.

There is a strong commitment to involving looked after young people on an authority-wide level. This has included: a young person's reference group for the Children's Services Plan; commissioning the children's rights officer and Who Cares? Scotland to consult with young people on the Best Value review on residential childcare; Who Cares? Scotland surveying educational issues for young people living away from home; and exploring the setting up of local support groups for looked after young people.

THROUGHCARE

Preparing young people for leaving care combines both individual and programme approaches. The review process and the use of the *Looking After Children* assessment and action records are central to planning and meeting individual needs. In addition, there is a planned throughcare programme for young people aged 14 to 16 living in children's homes. Although not described as a formal process, preparation is seen as part of the foster care role in relation to young people of this age group.

Young people are seen as active participants in the throughcare process, by their involvement in the planning process with their social worker and in attending reviews. This is part of a wider commitment to empowering young people through the employment of a children's rights officer by the authority and the involvement of young people in Who Cares? Scotland.

AFTERCARE

Personal support

Young people leaving care in the central and southern divisions will continue to be the responsibility of their area team social worker. In the north, the department have contracted the Barnardo's 16+ team to provide a specialist support service, although case responsibility is held by the social worker. In addition, reductions in the number of young people living in children's homes provided an opportunity for residential social workers to offer aftercare support to a small number of young people they had been looking after. In the Shire as a whole, area team social workers, specialist workers and residential workers are involved in providing individual personal support.

Barnardo's 16+ provides an outreach service in North Shire to young people who have been looked after or accommodated as well as other vulnerable young people referred by the department. They employ a project leader, four outreach workers and a housing development worker. As well as providing individual personal support, they have a project base, a drop-in service and offer short assured tenancies in partnership with a housing association. They receive 80 per cent of their funding (£164,000 a year in 2000–2001) from Shire Council.

Accommodation

As a joint service, social work and housing work collaboratively, as well as with other housing providers, to provide a range of accommodation options for care leavers. It is departmental policy that those in foster care can remain with carers beyond 18 if this is agreed by all key parties. Other provision throughout the county includes supported lodgings, a staffed hostel and staff-supported semi-independent flats, independent tenancies and a foyer. Young people's choices of type of accommodation and location are taken into account when planning accommodation, but it is not always possible to meet preferences given limitations on availability and locality including accessing support. Contingency arrangements include keeping beds available in foster and residential care on a short-term basis and integrated housing and social work policy and procedures in relation to all 16- and 17-year-olds presenting as homeless.

Financial assistance

Shire provides a leaving care grant of up to £1700 when young people leave care and up to £40 per week income supplementation for those aged 16 and 17. They may provide financial assistance to young people for further or higher education, accommodation subsidies or income 'top-up' payments. During 1999–2000 this sum totalled £75,185.50.

Education, employment and training

Helping young people with education, employment and training is built into the throughcare planning process and aftercare personal support.

Health and personal development

There are no specific initiatives targeted at young people leaving care in relation to sexual health and sexuality, drug and alcohol use, and leisure. However, during the course of the research a child and adolescent psychotherapy service dedicated to looked after children, including young people receiving aftercare, was introduced.

Monitoring and evaluation

Shire does not routinely collect statistical information on their throughcare and aftercare services but are intending to do so in the future. At the time of the research they were implementing the *Looking After Children* material, which has the potential to provide outcome data for all looked after young people. Outcome data is not collected on young people receiving aftercare services. Evaluation of throughcare and aftercare services includes inspection unit reports, Best Value reviews, annual reports from Shire's children's rights service and Who Cares? Scotland.

Conclusion

Our case study took place in three very different areas:

- County, having a specialist leaving care service that also includes a careers project to help young people access education, employment and training

- City, the largest urban centre in Scotland with the highest levels of unemployment and deprivation, which also has a specialist leaving care service that works in partnership with City's SIP to improve services for care leavers

- Shire, which has a non-specialist model provided by the joint housing and social work department that works with a Barnardo's 16+ team in one area.

These were our three areas and models of service provision for our study of young people leaving care. We will begin, in the next chapter, by introducing the young people and their experiences of care.

Notes

1 These names are used for anonymity.

2 Section 19 of the Children (Scotland) Act requires local authorities, in consultation with other relevant service providers, to prepare and publish Children's Services Plans for the provision of services for children and young people in their area. This presents an opportunity to provide a strategic focus for outlining services, objectives and priorities for developing throughcare and aftercare provision.

3 The *Looking After Children* (LAC) materials, which were developed in England, aim to improve the recording, assessing, planning and reviews process regarding children who are looked after away from home. They were adapted and introduced in Scotland in 1997.

Chapter 3

The Young People and their Experiences of Care

Introduction

Leaving care is both an individual and common journey. Young people leaving care each have their own characteristics and experiences. Each young person has his or her own story to tell. But it also possible to consider these young people as a group, who share common experiences. This chapter introduces the young people who took part in the study. It describes the general characteristics of the group, their care experience including their experience of education, and attempts to situate their characteristics and their experiences within the context of the national picture of living in and leaving care. We begin with a brief summary of the Scottish care context.

Around 11,400 children and young people are 'looked after' in care in Scotland (Scottish Executive 2003). These figures have remained fairly constant over recent years and represent around 1 per cent of the under-18 population.

Young people who are looked after in Scotland include those looked after under Section 70 of the Children (Scotland) Act 1995, either at home on a supervision requirement, or on a supervision requirement away from home in foster care or in residential care. Also included are those who are accommodated under Section 25 of the Children (Scotland) Act 1995, in either foster care or residential care.

Recent figures produced by the annual government review of local authorities show that almost half (48%) of looked after children and young people were looked after by their parents on a home supervision requirement. Meanwhile over a quarter (29%) were looked after away from home on supervision requirement and 12 per cent were accommodated under Section 25. Just over a quarter (27%) of all looked after children and young people were looked after in foster care and 14 per cent were in residential care (Scottish Executive 2001).

Young people who remain in care past the age of 15 are eligible for leaving care services under the Children (Scotland) Act 1995. This includes receiving ongoing throughcare services to prepare them for the time when they are no longer looked after and aftercare support to help them manage and sustain a smooth transition to post-care living, whether it be a return to the family home, semi or fully independent living or remaining with foster carers on an informal/non-statutory basis.

During the fieldwork timeframe of our research around 1300 young people left care in Scotland. Our study captures the experience of a relatively small but representative proportion (around 8% of the leaving care population) as they moved on from the care of three local authorities.

Describing the young people

One hundred and seven young people took part in the study. As outlined in Chapter 1, over half (57%) of these young people provided additional data by taking part in the follow-up study, six months on from the first contact. Information was gathered from young people themselves and, in most cases, also from their social worker or specialist leaving care worker (for simplicity, we shall in future refer to these people jointly as support workers and to specialist leaving care workers as leaving care workers). From this information we have been able to build up a basic demographic profile of care leavers from our three local authorities.

Local authority area

Over half (55%) of the group of young people in the study came from City authority, while almost a quarter (24%) came from County and a fifth (21%) from Shire. It is likely that we will see some area difference in young people's experience of care and leaving care. Although legislation has generally sought to standardise provision of support across area boundaries, local issues – such as resources, geography and wider socio-demographic factors – will inevitably come into play. For example, housing availability and options, the local labour market and access to services may impact upon a young person's life choices and chances however well prepared and supported they may be. We shall return to these issues in later chapters.

General characteristics

An exploration of the general characteristics of the group showed that a similar proportion of young men and young women participated in the study (49% and 51% respectively). The age at which they entered the study ranged from 15 to 20 years, although the average age of the group was 16½ years.

In terms of ethnicity, the vast majority (99%) of young people in our study described themselves as white, while the remaining 1 per cent described themselves as being of mixed origin. Recent figures produced by the Scottish Executive (2003) show that around 2 per cent of the looked after population come from minority ethnic groups so we can assume that our group was not too dissimilar from the national picture. Because of the small number of minority ethnic young people in our sample, it was not possible to explore further any specific issues that may have been related to ethnicity; however, it is an issue which demands greater attention.

In relation to health issues, over a tenth (14%) of young people entering the study reported having a long-term physical health problem, such as eczema, asthma, epilepsy and blood disorders, while almost a third (31%) reported learning difficulties. More apparent were difficulties related to mental health, emotional or behaviour difficulties, where support workers described around two in five young people (41%) as having such problems. In addition, although not necessarily a health issue, 5 per cent of those participating in the study considered themselves to be young disabled people.

Finally, parenthood was an issue for some young people in the group. Statistics show that Britain has the highest teenage conception rate of any European country (Social Exclusion Unit 1999) and figures published by the NHS in Scotland indicate that 7 per cent of all young women in the 16 to 19 age group living in Scotland experience pregnancy (NHS Scotland 2000).

Research into young people leaving care has highlighted the high incidence of teenage parenthood within this group (Biehal *et al.* 1992, 1995; Corlyon and McGuire 1997; Garnett 1992). In *Moving On*, for example, one half of young women in the follow-up sample had become parents by the age of 19 (Biehal *et al.* 1995).

At the point of entering our study over one in ten (12%) young people had a child and a further 4 per cent were (or had partners who were) pregnant. While most (57%) of these young people had become a parent at 16, over a quarter (29%) had entered parenthood at 15 years of age. Each young parent had one child only.

Just under half (43%) of the young parents described themselves as a 'lone parent', while two young people in the group were co-parents living together with their child. Over half (57%) of the young parents said that their child did not live with them; the majority of these were young men.

Research carried out in Scotland suggests a link between teenage pregnancy and deprivation, with the more deprived areas and urban areas having higher rates of conception and births (McLeod 2001). Our own study showed some difference in the rates of young parenthood across our three local authorities. The majority of young people who had a child came from City authority (67%), although proportionally County had the highest incidence of teenage parents (19%, compared to 16% in City). Shire, with its large rural band, had no teenage parents, although 16 per cent of the area sample were either pregnant or had a partner who was pregnant.

Joining the study

Young people were at various stages of their transition to post-care living when they joined the study. All had entered the study within 1 to 24 months of leaving care. Most young people (63%) entered the study within six months (the average), and most commonly within three months (the mode). All but 2 per cent entered the study within 18 months of moving on from care.

Young people were eligible to take part in the study providing they were eligible to receive throughcare and aftercare support under the Children (Scotland) Act 1995 (see Chapter 1). This included young people who were no longer looked after or accommodated and incorporated those who had legally left care (i.e. their supervision requirement had ended) and had moved on from a care placement to semi or independent living or had returned home. It also included those who had remained with foster carers after legal discharge from care and young people whose home supervision requirement had ended and who remained at home or had moved to semi/independent living.

Some young people, however, had moved on from care to semi/independent living while still legally looked after (i.e. on a supervision requirement). Such young people are also considered to have left care and were therefore included in our research.

Support workers were asked to specify the status of young people at the point of their referral to the study. As detailed in Table 3.1, over a third (37%) of young people entering the study were care leavers (either previously looked after at home or away from home) who had moved to independent living. Only 7 per cent had remained with their foster carer after being legally discharged from care and 15 per cent were young people who had moved on to independent living while still legally looked after. 'Other' included those who were homeless.

An area analysis carried out to explore whether certain status types were more prevalent in any of the three local authorities showed an association

between the young person's status at entry to the study and the local authority area from which they were recruited (p=0.003).

As Table 3.2 shows, very few young people from Shire had remained in
the family home (9%) and none of those looked after away from home had
returned home. Just under half (44%) of young people from City, however,
had either remained with (30%) or returned to the family (14%). The likelihood of remaining with foster carers after legal discharge also appeared to
differ according to the area. While 9 per cent of City young people and 9
per cent from Shire had remained with foster carers no one from County
had done so.

Table 3.1 Status of young people on entering the study

Status at entry to study	% of young people (n=107)
Care leaver returned to family home	13
Care leaver remaining in family home	24
Care leaver remaining with foster carer	7
Care leaver moved to independence	37
Looked after moved to independence	15
Other	4

Table 3.2 Percentage of young people per area in each status group

Status at entry to the study	% of total area sample		
	County	City	Shire
Care leaver returned to family home	23	14	0
Care leaver remaining in family home	23	30	9
Care leaver remaining with foster carers	0	9	9
Care leaver moved to independence	42	27	59
Looked after moved to independence	4	20	14
Other	8	0	9

The care experience

It is likely that a young person's experience of care will have some impact upon their abilities to manage the transition to post-care living. So, although the main focus of our research was on leaving care, we also gathered some background information on young people's care careers.

Some young people (at least 20%) in the study had entered care on more than one occasion. Information on the care episode prior to leaving care (i.e. the last care episode for those who had entered care several times and the only care episode for those who had come into care once only) was collected from their support worker. As outlined in Chapter 1, some support workers were unable to provide information and so data from workers generally refers to around 77 per cent of the total sample.

Legal status

Young people enter care for a number of reasons and accordingly will become looked after under a range of different legal requirements. Information on the legal status under which a young person was looked after during their last care episode is detailed in Table 3.3.

Table 3.3 Legal status of young people during last care episode

Legal status	% of young people (n=84)
Section 25	9
Placed in secure unit	3
Parental responsibilities order	5
Supervision order – residential school	5
Supervision order – residential unit	13
Supervision order – foster care	18
Supervision order – at home	30
Place of safety	4
Other (including no order)	13

National figures for the year up to March 2000 indicated that almost half (48%) of currently looked after young people were on a supervision requirement at home (Scottish Executive 2001). In our survey of young people who had left care, just under a third (30%) of those for whom we have information had been looked after on home supervision during their last care episode. This reflects the national picture where home supervision requirements are the most common form of care in Scotland.

Support workers were also asked to indicate the main reason for the young person becoming looked after during their last care episode. The most common reason, as shown in Table 3.4, was 'parents unable to provide care' (31%). Reasons included in the 'Other' category were death of parents, family rejection, and sex offences committed by the young person.

Care placements

Most young people, as we shall see later, experience more than one care placement. Information on their initial and final placement was collected. This provided some insight into the range, and number, of placements young people had experienced before leaving care.

Table 3.4 Reasons for entering last care episode

Reason for being looked after	% of young people (n=84)
Substance misuse	1
Offending	8
School non-attendance	15
Moral danger	1
Beyond control	23
Schedule 1 offender in the home	1
Victim of sexual or physical abuse	13
Parents unable to provide care	31
Other	7

Initial placements

Data on initial placements showed that the majority of young people had been placed away from home with almost a third (32%) being placed in foster care, 22 per cent in children's homes and 7 per cent in residential schools. Less than a tenth (5%) had been placed with other relatives while a similar proportion (7%) had been initially placed in other accommodation, such as secure units, assessment centres and a residential reception unit. Over a quarter (27%) of the group had been looked after in the family home.

Analysis showed that there was some difference in the extent to which the different local authority areas utilised different types of care placements (p=0.001). This will of course be influenced to some extent by differences in supply and resources. For example, some areas will have access to more residential units and others may be struggling to maintain a supply of foster carers.

Most young people from County and Shire had been placed in foster homes (41% and 68% respectively). In comparison, only a tenth (11%) of young people from City had been placed with foster carers. Being placed with family on a home supervision requirement accounted for over a third (35%) of young people from County and over a quarter (29%) of young people from City.

There has generally been a decrease in the use of residential care in recent years. This has come about as a result of poor outcomes identified in research findings, revelations of abuse in residential care, as well as concerns over the high costs of such placements (Frost *et al.* 1999). Residential placements, however, were very apparent in City with a third (34%) of young people from the area having been placed in residential care compared to 6 per cent in County and 11 per cent in Shire. In fact, all young people who had initially been placed in a residential unit came from City authority.

Last placement

Information on young people's last placement before moving on from care showed that most young people had been looked after within the family home (32%) or with foster carers (29%). A small proportion (8%) of young people had lived with other relatives, such as grandparents and aunts, prior to moving on from care and 21 per cent had moved on from residential care, either from a school (11%) or a children's unit (10%). A tenth (10%) of young people in the sample had left care from other placements, such secure units, independence training flats or 16+ units.

Length of time in care

Some young people enter care for a short period of time while others will spend a considerable part of their childhood in care, entering as young children and remaining until they are young adults. The average age at which young people in the group had entered their last care episode was 13 years. The majority (68%) were in fact aged 14 or over.

Young people in the study had been looked after from between one month and 16 years prior to moving on or being discharged from care. Just over a quarter (28%) of young people had spent three or more years in care during their last care episode. Those who had experienced more than one care episode will have spent more time in care in total. The average length of time in care during the last care episode was 33 months.

Placement moves

As indicated earlier, most young people move placements during their care career. Previous research has certainly highlighted the tendency for looked after young people to experience movement and disruption in their lives (Biehal *et al.* 1995; Stein 1990) and has emphasised the importance of striving for continuity and stability in care as a basis for promoting positive life chances after care.

In the current study, the average number of placement moves during the last care episode only (not the care career) was two. Indeed the majority (65%) of young people had experienced two moves or less; however, the number of placement moves experienced by the group ranged from none to 15 moves.

Young people looked after at home on a supervision requirement were more likely to remain looked after within the home and were therefore less likely to experience movement. We therefore temporarily removed those who had been looked after at home from our analysis so that we could focus more closely on the placement movement of those who had been looked after away from home. Results indicated that the average number of placement moves for the remaining young people (n=57) rose to three moves during the last care episode. Furthermore, only 7 per cent of those who had been placed away from home had in fact remained in the same care placement throughout their last care episode. Most young people had experienced some instability, with a third having moved on at least four occasions.

There was no significant relationship between the number of placement moves experienced by young people placed away from home and either their local authority area or their gender. There was, however, evidence of a correlation between the number of placement moves experienced by young people placed away from home and the length of time they had been looked after during their last care episode.[1]

Analysis showed that, on average, young people placed away from home had been looked after for 38 months. With the average number of placement moves for this group totalling three, some of these young people may have moved on average at least once per year.

The importance of placement stability is demonstrated by theories related to child development, such as attachment theory. This suggests that a child's emotional development is best facilitated by a close and consistent relationship with an adult who can provide care, comfort, guidance and protection. In the absence of such a relationship the child may suffer emotional damage which can result in feelings of low self-esteem, distrust of others, difficulties in forming relationships and, in extreme cases, anger and anti-social behaviour. As has been demonstrated by previous research and practice-based evidence, and is echoed by our own research, those young people who have experienced greater stability in their care careers are more likely to make a smooth transition to adulthood (Stein 2004). That is to say, they will have more positive outcomes across a range of life areas, including employment, housing, social relationships and, as we shall see in the following section, education (Department of Health 1998).

The education of young people in care

> It is unacceptable if that by being in care children get a poorer start in life; some of our most vulnerable young people are not being supported by the formal education system. (Jack McConnell, then Minister for Education, Europe and External Affairs, BBC News Scotland March 2001)

As Mr McConnell's comments imply, looked after young people and young people leaving care have lower levels of educational attainment and participation rates than young people in the general population. This may be the result of the complex inter-relationship between social deprivation (structural and cultural factors), damaging pre-care family experiences and the difficulties which led them into care, all of which may impact upon their educational performance (Bynner and Parsons 2002; Cheung and Heath 1994; Coleman, Hofler and Kilgore 1981; Jackson 2001; Stein 1994). However, that looked after young people are persistently failing to reach their full potential has raised the possibility that the care experience itself can serve to exacerbate pre-care educational difficulties rather than compensate for them. There has been a growing awareness that placement instability and the lack of emphasis placed upon education by care workers and carers have reinforced the barriers to education faced by these young people (Jackson 2001).

Recent studies undertaken by Barnardo's across Scotland, England and Wales (Barnardo's 2001) and by the HM Inspectors of Schools and the Social Work Services Inspectorate in Scotland have highlighted the need for better working structures and cooperation between agencies to promote and support the education of looked after young people. In *Learning with Care* (HM Inspectors of Schools and the Social Work Services Inspectorate 2001) findings confirmed that, compared to their non-care peers, young people looked after away from home in five Scottish local authorities tended to be behind in their attainments, leave school with fewer qualifications and have a greater risk of being excluded. A similar picture emerged from our own findings.

Information on the educational attainment and achievement of young people in the current study was sought from workers and young people themselves. Over a quarter of workers who returned a questionnaire stated that they did not know whether the young person they were working with had any qualifications at the point of moving on from care. This was a concerning finding, given the importance of education in post-care planning. The following information is based solely on young persons' data.

At the point of entry to the current study six (5%) young people were still at school. Only one of these had (at 17 years of age) continued past compulsory education. The vast majority of the young people in the study (95%) had left school and many had done so without qualifications.

Educational attainment

Although some young people succeed and indeed excel in their education while looked after, evidence from previous research suggests that overall the educational outcomes for looked after young people have been consistently poor (Stein 2004). In Biehal's survey of English care leavers, half of the follow-up sample had no qualifications (Biehal *et al.* 1995), while more recently *Learning with Care* reported that up to 75 per cent of looked after young people across five Scottish authorities had left school without any qualifications.

Young people in our study were asked to list their qualifications. Fewer than half (39%) reported having one or more standard grades.[2] The majority (61%) did not have any. These figures, while disconcerting, mirror the current national picture for Scottish care leavers, which show that 60 per cent of young people leave care without any standard grade qualifications (Scottish Executive 2003). The extent to which these young people are disadvantaged educationally is made particularly apparent when we compare them to young people in general. Data collected by the Scottish Executive for the same year as the research shows that only 5 per cent of all school leavers in Scotland had no qualifications (Scottish Executive 2003). Furthermore, in comparison to the national average of seven standard grades at any level (HM Inspectorate 2001) the average number of standard grades in our study was two.

The picture is a little less discouraging, however, when we focus on the relatively small number of young people in the study who had succeeded in their education. For those who did have standard grades, the average was four, and more than a quarter (29%) had left school with between seven and nine standard grade qualifications. Additionally, a small proportion of young people (3%) had achieved between one and three Highers. However, this compares to almost a third (30%) of the general population of Scottish school leavers who go on to achieve Higher qualifications (Scottish Executive 2000b).

Ministerial concerns about educational attainment of those leaving care are reflected in the social justice milestones, which set the target that, 'all our young people leaving local authority care will have achieved at least English and Maths standard grades' (Scottish Executive 2000c). In the current study just over a third of the group said they had achieved a standard grade in Maths (35%) and in English (39%). Again these figures are broadly representative of the national picture of care leavers which shows that around 27 per cent had achieved standard grade Maths and English but compare poorly to the 91 per cent of school leavers in the general population who achieve standard grades in these subjects (Scottish Executive 2002, 2003).

While these findings clearly show that looked after young people, and those leaving care, generally fare worse in education than their non-care peers, they also show that some do succeed. Analysis was carried out to explore whether there were any patterns within the data to suggest which young people were likely to do better or worse in terms of education attainment and what factors may help them to succeed.

There was some indication that females tended to do better than males. Almost twice as many young women had standard grades when compared to young men in the group (63% and 36% respectively). We also found that around half (52%) of those who had one or more standard grades had left care from a foster placement (p=0.014). This does have some resonance with existing UK research which has shown that young women who have been looked after in stable foster care placements tend to do better educationally than other looked after young people (Biehal *et al.* 1995; Social Exclusion Unit 2003).

A further factor to arise from existing research into the difficulties facing looked after young people is the disruption and interruption of schooling caused by placement movement. Stability of placement may therefore be a factor in enhancing the educational chances of looked after young people. Analysis carried out of the sample as a whole implied no relationship between educational attainment and placement moves during the young person's last care episode. However, when we focused on those who had been looked after away from home we found a negative correlation between the number of placement moves and the number of qualifications achieved, suggesting that those who had moved more often had fewer standard grades.[3] This was further demonstrated when we looked at all those young people who had one or more standard grades. Here we found a negative correlation between the number of qualifications achieved and the number of placement moves they had experienced.[4] This indicates that those who had achieved a greater number of standard grades had experienced fewer placement moves while in care and provides a clear message that stability in care can facilitate educational attainment.

The importance of education, however, is not only evidenced through attainment. Attending school is an essential part of a child's development necessary for acquiring skills in communication, social interaction and developing and negotiating relationships. School can also provide a source of structure and stability for a young person whose life is otherwise uncertain or troubled. Importantly it may also provide a basis for developing confidence and positive self-esteem through academic and also non-academic awards and activities, such as sport, drama or practical courses. Indeed, many (63%) young people in the study told us of certificates for sports, first aid courses and recreational activities, which, while not indicative of academic accomplishment, nevertheless represented a sense of achievement. It is crucial therefore that looked after young people are assisted to participate in education with as little interruption and as few difficulties as possible.

Education participation and exclusion

In terms of educational participation and exclusion, *Learning with Care* (HM Inspectorate 2001) reported that looked after children account for 1 per cent of the school population and yet they make up 13 per cent of all school exclusions. Almost three quarters (72%) of young people in our study reported having been either temporarily or permanently excluded. Many young people told us they had lost count of the number of 'suspensions' they had and many felt that it had been for 'daft things', such as spitting in the playground or not doing homework. Lyn, a young woman who had been suspended on at least four occasions, told us:

> I didn't take school seriously, I was a wee rebel but half the things you got suspended for were just stupid. I struggled a lot, I think because of my past. I didn't like adults speaking back to me so was cheeky back. I've learned

obviously. It wasn't until 5th or 6th year that I started thinking about my education.

Truancy was also common amongst young people in the study with 83 per cent having stayed off school at some point and 51 per cent having done so 'often'. As noted earlier, however, around a tenth of the sample had become looked after because of school non-attendance. As Rory commented, 'I went for weeks without going to school, that's how I got stuck in a home.'

Some young people truanted because of problems they were experiencing at school. Lyn explained, '[from] 2nd to 4th year, I found the work difficult and didn't want to be at school. It was difficult coz I'd missed a lot of schooling'. Amanda, who had experienced several placement moves and subsequently had also moved school on a number of occasions, highlighted the difficulties of settling in. She told us she truanted because 'I was new at school and didn't feel comfortable.' Gordon, who truanted 'all the time', indicated the lack of support he had received to overcome his learning difficulties:

> I stayed off a lot, all the time. I was dyslexic. It was hard in English being told to stand up and read when you couldn't read or write properly...it was known since I was in primary school but when I went to high school I didn't get any support.

Several young people expressed regret at having truanted, as in the following comments from Ivan and Jessica: 'I [truanted] sometimes a couple of days at a time, sometimes two weeks. I regret it now and wish I'd stuck in at school but I couldn't spell properly and had difficulty with reading.' Jessica, meanwhile, had truanted often and left school without any qualifications. She told us, 'I regret it now...if I'd gone to school I'm sure I would have achieved really good grades. I'm not stupid.'

None of the above young people had achieved any qualifications at the time of providing the information. However, on a more positive note, one young woman told us that she had truanted while living at home but 'I never did it in care...my school attendance improved when I was in care'. She had gone on to complete eight standard grades all at grades three and four.

School difficulties

As we have seen, a number of young people experienced difficulties with their schooling. In addition to the problems with literacy, concentration and dyslexia outlined above, 7 per cent were reported to have had a statement or record of special educational needs. Some young people commented on the lack of support they had received to address their difficulties. One young person told us they were dyslexic but did not receive any support – 'My mum went off her head trying to get me support but I still didn't get any' – and Justin said he had trouble with writing but didn't know how to get any help; he added, 'I was scared of what people thought.' A further problem for some young people in the study was the experience of being bullied. Although most (57%) young people told us they had never been bullied, over a quarter (29%) said they had been bullied at some point and for 14 per cent this had happened often. Many of these young people described instances of name-calling and intimidation. Unsurprisingly, experiences of being bullied could lead to truanting and subsequent exclusion, and for some it was linked directly to being in care. Josh, who had attended a residential school, told us:

> I was bullied often, when I was younger…it's part of it really, when you go in till you get a bit bigger. I was in two residential schools, I would say the first one I was 13…it happened for about four months.

Mandy, who had been suspended for not wearing her school uniform, explained that being bullied had resulted in her being excluded from school. She commented:

> When I was in homes they didn't buy me good stuff to wear so I got bullied for that so I wouldn't wear [the uniform]. I was suspended six or seven times within a couple of years.

Findings from this and previous research highlight the need for improving the educational experience of looked after young people, in terms of increasing attainment and addressing educational needs and the causes of truancy and exclusion. A further priority, as illustrated by the closing comment from a young person who took part in the study, is to raise awareness amongst social workers, teachers and carers to ensure that those more closely involved in the care of young people fulfil their role in promoting education and facilitating those in their care to reach their full educational potential:

> I get angry at my parents and social workers for not pushing me in my education. I feel that if I'd stuck in at school, if I'd got the right education at the right time, I could have really gone further and got a really good job. I'm angry at other folk about that because I feel I missed a lot of education and it's so unfair for me.

Involving young people

With the exception of education, we have so far described young people's care experience through the use of information largely derived from the collation of case file data provided via their support worker. While this type of information sets the general context for understanding their experience, it is only by listening to the views of young people that we can get a true sense of what it is like to be looked after in care.

This next section explores young people's views and experiences of being looked after in care. First, how did the local authorities we surveyed (31 in all) facilitate the process of listening to young people and how did they ensure their participation in the development of services and policy?

Involving young people in the planning and review of throughcare and aftercare services is important on several accounts: it engenders a sense of ownership amongst services users; it presents service providers with a means of identifying need and assessing the effectiveness of services in meeting those needs; and it upholds the rights of young people as outlined in the Children (Scotland) Act 1995. Overall, we found that local authorities in Scotland were committed to facilitating the participation of young people in all aspects of the service planning and review process.

Development of policies, procedures and guidance

Over three-quarters (n=24) of authorities said that they had arrangements for involving looked after young people and care leavers in the development of their policy, procedures and guidance. Young people appeared to play a significant role in the consultation process for their Children's Services Plans and three authorities reported that recent surveys of young people had been conducted as a means of evaluating throughcare and aftercare services. Further examples included young person's consultation groups, working groups which included service user involvement, youth forums, youth groups linked to Social Inclusion Partnerships and close links with Who Cares? Scotland.

Throughcare process

Young people were encouraged to participate in the planning of their own throughcare process through consultation and attendance at care planning and review meetings. Several authorities reported that advocacy via children's rights officers and Who Cares? workers was available to facilitate the process.

Reviews

Ensuring that young people were fully involved in the review process involved similar measures across all authorities. Most highlighted the importance of preparing the young person for the review and making them feel comfortable with the procedures. Some examples included: providing them with a 'user friendly' review report prior to the review; providing easy-to-understand information leaflets that outlined the purpose of the review; assistance in writing their own reports either by staff, Who Cares? workers or children's rights officers; and informal discussions between young people and relevant workers to ensure that their needs and wishes were identified.

Monitoring and evaluation

Over two-thirds of authorities (n=21) said that young people's views were incorporated into the monitoring and evaluation process for throughcare and aftercare services. This was largely achieved by consultation in the preparation of Children's Services Plans, involvement in focus or screening groups, routine consultation on various issues, 'client' questionnaires and participating in youth forums. Two of the authorities that do not currently have such procedures in place commented that progress was being made in this area.

Young people's views of care

This final section turns to young people's own views of their care experience; we asked young people who had been looked after away from home to highlight some of the good things and bad things about being in care. Not surprisingly, experiences were mixed, both within and across cases.

What are the good things?

When asked 'What are the good things about being in care?' most young people were able to identify positive aspects and experiences. Most commonly these included having company and comfort, as Lewis indicated: 'It was having people there when I needed them.' Having someone to talk to, or someone who understood and had shared similar experiences, was also valued by Ellie, who told us, 'I could speak quite freely, there was always someone to talk to', and also by Alan, who felt that there were 'people I could talk to, people who understood me who could listen to me and help me'.

Feelings of safety, belonging and being supported were also common themes amongst young people's responses. Susan noted, 'The good things were a bit of security with staff there all the time and I could relate to the other young persons in the unit', and Tony, whose last placement was with foster carers, summed up the good aspects as the feeling that 'I was safe, I could talk about my problems. I was looked after properly. I was loved.'

The importance of stability was also touched upon. For example, Laura, who had experienced two foster placements, told us that the good things were 'having a very stable environment where you can be at ease and have people to talk to when you need help. Also, the longer you stay in care the more you feel part of the family'.

The idea of escape from a troubled situation also emerged. Emma told us, 'It's really good, escaping one situation and going into a more stable home environment. Foster carers are brilliant and treat you as one of the family.' Similarly, Jay, who had been through a difficult time at home before coming into care, told us, 'When I was in care I was well away from that bastard of a stepfather my mother had the misfortune to marry.'

For some young people, the move into a stable and supportive care environment had facilitated their personal development. In addition to the positive effects of feeling safe, at ease, wanted and understood, young people also described changes in their self-confidence and ability to overcome their difficulties and develop their interpersonal skills. Shona had lived with her foster carers for four years. She told us: 'My foster family was more settled than home and I managed to becomes less introverted while in care.' Fran identified the positive aspects of building a social network while living in residential care: 'You get to know staff and friends really well, you get a relationship with them and learn how to communicate.' Some young people talked of the personal support they had received from carers whether it was being 'talked to as an adult', helped to address difficulties or simply having some time and space to reflect and develop, as in Joseph's case. 'My foster carers were cool people and I got on well with them. They helped me with my trouble – encouraged me to share my problems – it gave me time to think about things and how I could change.'

Young people also talked about the material and social advantages of being looked after in care. For some, care may have presented positive opportunities that they might otherwise not have had. Most often young people highlighted having holidays or day trips out, getting money for new clothes or pursuing hobbies and leisure activities. For a few like Max, this also involved educational opportunities. He told us the good thing about care was: 'It gave me the chance to get an education.'

What are the bad things?

Amongst some of the negative aspects of being looked after were feelings of isolation; most commonly this involved feeling cut off from family and friends. Many young people expressed similar sentiments to Emma:

> No matter who your family are you are going to miss them from time to time, no matter you feel rejected and you resent that. At times you wonder whether they [foster carers] want you or is it just a job, not that mine were like that, but some.

Emma's comment highlights the dilemma many young people face as they come to terms with being in care. Another common issue was the feeling of being labelled or discriminated against. Several young people commented on the difficulties of dealing with preconceptions. For Owen, one of the bad things about being in care was that 'people thought I had done something wrong' and Lewis told us the worst thing was 'being accused of things I hadn't done by the public, getting hassled by them. The assumptions they made'.

A lack of 'privacy' and feelings of being punished or imprisoned were also experienced. Andy, for example, felt he was being 'held like a prisoner' and Brian said that the bad things included being 'restrained by staff'. He told us, 'Even if it was the best place I would still have hated it because it was not home.'

Other restrictions, such as not having the freedom to make decisions or contact relatives and friends and 'sticking to the rules given', were also mentioned. Rona felt that:

> The most bad thing about being in care was being so far away from home and not being able to see your family when you wanted. You were only allowed to contact them when they [staff] said you were.

Difficulties with carers or with other young people were also amongst the negative experiences of care. Helen told us that her experience of foster care involved 'regular fall-outs with the other girls which made me feel awkward as I had to share a room'. She added, 'and the carer always took his own family's side which I don't think was fair, they should have made everyone equal'. Lucy, who had been in residential care, told us that 'there was some bullying by the older ones and the way some of the staff spoke – treated me sometimes – they could be nasty'. There was also evidence of the negative effects of peer pressure. Fran told us: 'You get to know other people who have done something else bad and you get to know what they do and you stay with them and they drag you with them.' For Stewart, the bad thing about care was that 'I learned bad habits [and] got involved with offending.'

Overall, most young people were able to draw on both positive and negative features of the care experience. Sharon, who had moved five times, summed up her experience of care in terms of the good and bad aspects:

> You know you will be looked after if your own parents can't look after you properly. Leaving care and social work [staff] try to make sure you don't have a hard time of it, but there's not a lot of choice about where you go and a lot of moving around. Children's homes can sometimes get over-crowded and people tend to discriminate against you when they find out you were in foster care.

Conclusion

This chapter has introduced the young people taking part in the study. It has explored their general characteristics and has focused on both the collective and individual experience of being looked after within the Scottish care system. Generally, the emerging picture of the care experience for young people leaving care in Scotland appeared to be consistent with those experiences documented in previous research into looked after children and young people leaving care. We have seen that these young people are a diverse group with a range of needs and experiences. Most move on to independent living earlier than other young people and many will have experienced disruption in their accommodation and their education while looked after. As highlighted in young people's own accounts of care, many miss their family and friends and there was an appreciation of the support they had received from foster or residential carers and support workers.

The messages to arise out of these experiences are important ones for those involved in developing and providing care services for these young people – from policy makers to carers. For example, the importance of ongoing family contact where appropriate cannot be underestimated. Nor can the need for suitable and stable care placements or for support to identify and address risk factors and individual needs, including health care and education.

In exploring the characteristics and experiences of this group of young people, this chapter has set the context for their experience of moving on from care and has identified some of the key factors (e.g. age, placement stability, education) which may have influenced their decisions, progress and life chances after care. These key factors will be drawn upon throughout the following chapters as we explore outcomes for young people leaving care and begin to look in more detail at what promotes positive outcomes and experiences during the transition to post-care independent living.

Notes

1 The test result was Kendall's tau b=0.238, p=0.017.

2 Standard grades are the Scottish equivalent to the GCSE qualification taken by pupils in England and Wales. Standard grades are generally taken over the third and fourth years at secondary school, with an exam at the end of the fourth year. Students often take seven or eight subjects, including Maths and English. There are three levels of study: Credit, General, and Foundation. Highers (the Scottish Higher Grade Certificate) are recognised as entrance qualifications to universities. Unlike the A-level course in England and Wales, Highers take one year to complete.

3 The test result was Kendall's tau b=-0.319, p=0.010.

4 The test result was Kendall's tau b=-0.316, p=0.018.

Chapter 4

Throughcare: Preparation for Leaving Care

Introduction

So far we have described young people's general experience of being looked after in care – where they were looked after, how long they were in care, their education and what they viewed as the good and bad things about care. As we shall see in later chapters, many aspects of the care experience are likely to impact upon a young person's life chances after they leave care. One of the more fundamental aspects, however, is the help they receive to develop the skills to prepare them for adulthood.

In this chapter we focus specifically on the process of preparing young people for leaving care. In doing so we look at local authority policy and practice procedures for providing preparation. We also explore what preparation involves, who helps and how well prepared young people felt and were seen to be by their support workers. But, first, what do we mean by preparation?

Preparation

Preparation for adult life involves the development of skills that enable us to look after ourselves physically and emotionally and enable us to participate in our social environment.

For most young people, preparation for adult life is a gradual process beginning in childhood and progressing steadily in accordance with increasing age and personal development. It is a supported process, usually taking place within the family arena and is participatory by nature involving discussion – or argument – as well as negotiation, risk taking, making mistakes and trying again. It is also holistic in approach, affording equal importance to the development of practical, emotional and interpersonal skills (Stein and Wade 2000). This is the challenge facing the corporate parents of looked after young people as they help them to prepare for independent adult living.

In Scotland, the requirement to prepare young people for the time they are no longer looked after is contained within the principle of 'throughcare'. This chapter draws upon national policy data to explore the extent to which Scottish local authorities are facilitating the throughcare process via their policy and development frameworks. It will then look at how throughcare is working in practice by drawing on the experiences of young people from our three Scottish authorities, who have been through the important stage of preparation for independent adult living.

Throughcare in Scotland

> Throughcare is the process by which the local authority plans and prepares the young person they are looking after for the time when he or she will cease to be looked after. (The Children (Scotland) Act 1995 Regulations and Guidance, Vol. 2)

As laid down in the Guidance, when young people enter their teenage years their preparation should become more structured and formal. In our policy survey of 31 authorities, most (77%) reported having a planned throughcare programme for young people. Almost a quarter (23%), however, did not. Some authorities operated their own eligibility criteria and as such their throughcare provision was restricted to certain groups of the looked after population.

We found that young people looked after in children's homes were eligible in all authorities that operated a planned throughcare programme, and young people in foster care were eligible in as many as 83 per cent of these authorities. Young people placed with parents or family, however, were eligible for planned throughcare in less than half of the authorities who had such programmes (46%). Just under a quarter of the authorities extended their planned throughcare programme to 'other groups' of young people, including those looked after in secure units or in youth custody, homeless young people and young people referred from other authorities. One authority added that in 'in cases of extreme vulnerability throughcare will be allocated to other groups including looked after at home'.

The most common age for young people to begin a planned throughcare programme was 15 years old (58% of authorities). One authority respondent said it depended on the circumstances of the young person. The programmes tend to be incorporated into young people's care plans via throughcare plans and reviews and the *Looking After Children* (LAC) reviews.[1] Timing of reviews varied from weekly or fortnightly to every three months.

As highlighted above, preparing young people for the transition to adulthood and independent living should attach equal importance to practical, emotional and interpersonal skills. The following five elements have been suggested as integral to an effective preparation programme: self-care skills (personal hygiene, diet and health, including sexual health); practical skills (budgeting, shopping, cooking, cleaning); interpersonal skills (managing a range of formal and informal relationships, including sexual relationships); education (planning and supporting positive progress); and identity (knowledge of and links with family and community, sexuality, cultural knowledge/skills for young people from ethnic minorities) (Stein and Wade 2000).

We asked authorities to outline the main areas covered by their throughcare programme. We then matched their responses to the five areas described above. This provided us with some indication of how comprehensive their throughcare programmes were. Table 4.1 illustrates those areas that were specifically mentioned in the programme outlines.

Table 4.1 Areas covered by throughcare programmes in 21 authorities

Areas	Authorities that covered these areas
Self-care	11
Practical skills	16
Interpersonal skills	12
Education	11
Identity	1

Of the 24 authorities that said they offered planned throughcare programmes, three did not supply us with details of the areas covered. Of the 21 who did supply an outline, only one authority mentioned all five preparation areas. Three authorities mentioned four areas while the majority of local authorities with a planned preparation programme (71%) mentioned three areas or less. In six authorities additional areas – such as leisure, benefit entitlements, accessing help/social support, accommodation, personal safety and counselling – were covered in the throughcare programme. Also, a number of authorities did report that they were in the process of implementing the LAC material and would be addressing the seven dimensions contained within it.

Overall, we found that practical skills and interpersonal skills were covered by most authorities; however, identity was mentioned by only one.

Some young people will have specific needs which should be addressed in their throughcare planning. In some cases special provision may be necessary. We found that 55 per cent of authorities offered specific provision to one or more groups of the looked after population, who may have particular needs (see Table 4.2).

Table 4.2 Authorities with specific throughcare provision

Looked after sub-groups	Number of authorities with specific provision (n=31)
Young people from minority ethnic backgrounds	3
Young parents	10
Physically disabled young people	6
Learning disabled young people	7
Young people with mental health problems	11
Young people with substance misuse problems	10
Young offenders	12

Some of the authorities that did not have specific throughcare provision stated that special needs were addressed on an individual basis and staff would attempt to identify relevant support.

Leaving care planning
Looking After Children records
The *Looking After Children* (LAC) assessment and action records provide a framework for approaching throughcare planning and review. We found that 42 per cent of the responding authorities were currently using the LAC material. A further 23 per cent reported that they were either in the process of implementing the records or were planning to implement them. Eleven (35%) authorities said they were not using the records.

Leaving care review

Most of the authorities (84%) said that their leaving care policies and procedures included a requirement to hold a leaving care review. A further two commented that there was no specific requirement to hold a review but it was normal practice to do so. Of the remaining authorities, two said that they had no specific leaving care reviews, 'rather they are incorporated into normal reviews'.

Most authorities responded that all relevant persons were invited to attend reviews. The general consensus was that reviews should be sensitive to who should attend by balancing the young person's wishes with the relevant contribution of others. This could include specialist workers or representatives from relevant agencies, such as education or health services. Several authorities mentioned the involvement of workers from Who Cares? Scotland. We also found that leaving care reviews (and childcare reviews in general) were used as a means of promoting and encouraging family contact, where appropriate.

AREAS COVERED IN THE REVIEW

The planning and review process prior to a young person leaving care is the foundation upon which good aftercare support can be built (Stein and Wade 2000). It is important, therefore, that a wide range of issues is addressed during the leaving care review. It has been suggested (First Key 1996) that the following areas should be considered during the leaving care planning and review:

1. Safe affordable accommodation options appropriate to the young person's needs, taking account of location and support networks; financial assistance to set up and maintain the accommodation.

2. Education, employment and training options; financial assistance where required.

3. Assistance with claiming entitlement to welfare benefits, where appropriate.

4. Provision of general and specialised health care.

5. Leisure options.

6. Maintenance of informal networks of support, including family members and friends; creation of new networks of advice and support, where appropriate.

7. Introduction to specialist services where appropriate (counselling, advocacy, health).

8. Clear signposting of sources of assistance in the future, including out of hours in emergency.

Authorities were asked to identify the main areas covered in their leaving care reviews. Their responses were matched to the above category areas. Table 4.3 shows which of these categories were mentioned by the 28 authorities that held leaving care reviews and supplied details of their review areas.

Table 4.3 Areas covered in reviews by local authorities

Review areas	1	2	3	4	5	6	7	8
% of authorities covering review areas (n=28)	54	64	43	43	7	50	7	32

Other areas mentioned in the outlines included recent progress and work required, issues related to offending, future plans, the seven LAC dimensions, welfare rights, risk assessment, emotional matters, throughcare plan and objectives achieved.

Twenty-seven authorities outlined their procedures for monitoring and recording review decisions. Forty-one per cent of these mentioned the use of LAC material to monitor decisions and 7 per cent used throughcare monitoring forms. Decisions tended to be recorded via the process of taking minutes and distributing them to relevant parties.

Young people's experience of throughcare

As well as our policy survey, information on throughcare support was collected from support workers and young people in our three authorities. It indicated that only two-fifths (40%) of young people in the study had received a planned programme of preparation. The majority (60%) had not.

Before looking in more detail at young people's experience of throughcare support it is worth first considering the reasons why less than half of the study sample had received planned support. Support workers were asked to indicate why young people had not received a formal programme of preparation support. Reasons varied, but generally fell into four main categories.

1. Unable to engage with support

Some young people had been unwilling or unable to engage in a through-care programme. Comments from workers suggested that this could be because of a young person's particular circumstances. For example, one worker said of the young person she worked with: 'He was very depressed and refused or was unable to comply [with the support programme].' In other cases, the young person did not want help from throughcare services. One support worker commented that: 'A planned programmed was pre-pared but my client would not participate regardless of any amount of encouragement. He did not wish a service and did not read the life skills pack.' Another told us, 'Nicola refused all contact despite [my] attempts. She was adamant that she did not need throughcare support.'

2. An unplanned or early move from care

A number of young people had moved on from care sooner than anticipated either by choice or because of placement breakdown. For some, this had taken place before a formal preparation programme could be implemented or completed. For example, one support worker noted that the young person he was working with had not received any planned preparation because 'she absconded prior to her care order being terminated and [before] any formal programme to assist her in becoming more independent could be instigated'. Another worker commented that 'the [preparation] programme started within residential school but was discontinued due to [the young person's] behaviour and he was asked to leave'. Several workers also commented on the timing of their involvement with young people. One told us, 'Throughcare [services] only got involved after the foster place-ment broke down', and another said, 'A referral to throughcare was only made five weeks before the placement was ending so some prep was carried out by the foster carers.'

3. No formal programme of preparation available

As reported in our policy survey, some local authorities had not developed a planned programme of preparation support. In our three case study authori-ties it appeared that some young people had not received a planned programme of preparation because no such programme had been offered. Indeed one worker commented, 'there was no formal plan available at the time'.

4. Local eligibility criteria

We also found some evidence to suggest that certain groups of young people had not been offered a planned programme of support. This was disconcerting, as the Children (Scotland) Act 1995 envisages that throughcare should be available to all looked after young people. However, as discussed earlier in the chapter, our national survey of Scottish local authorities indicated that some were operating their own local eligibility criteria for providing formal preparation support. This finding was also evident in analysis of our three case study areas. For example, comments from support workers suggested that young people who were looked after at home and those returning home were considered either not eligible for throughcare services or only eligible in the event of a crisis. One worker stated, 'The throughcare [team] were not approached as he continued to reside at home with relatives.' Another told us: 'She returned to the parental home when her placement broke down and throughcare would have only been undertaken in a crisis or breakdown of home placement.' This was supported by further analysis, which showed that only a fifth of young people who had been looked after at home had received a planned programme of preparation compared to almost two-fifths (38%) of those in foster care and half of young people placed in residential units.

Although over half of the sample had not received a planned programme of support, it was apparent that many young people had received some informal or ad hoc preparation. Most often this had been undertaken by carers or family members while the young person was looked after or by support workers or carers after the young person had left care.

Delivering planned preparation

For those young people who had received planned preparation (40%), the programme tended to begin around the mid-teens with most (52%) beginning the programme at 16 years of age (the average age of leaving care) and a further third beginning at 15. A small proportion of young people, however, had not received planned support until relatively late into their teens (e.g. 17 and 18) and for some it had taken place after they had left care. As we have already seen, planning the timing of preparation support is important. Some support workers identified the dilemma of introducing preparation for independent living too soon as they felt that this might indirectly encourage young people to leave care early, while beginning a planned programme later ran the risk of young people leaving care without being adequately prepared. This perhaps emphasises the need for a gradual and intrinsic process of life skills acquisition, which, while planned and monitored, is incorporated into the young person's care plan from the point of entry to care. In this sense, preparation should not be left until the throughcare team become involved, nor should it consist of a crash course in independent living skills a few months prior to a young person's exit from care.

Who helped?

Providing throughcare support appeared to involve a collaborative approach. Support workers identified a range of people and services that were involved in delivering throughcare to those young people who had received a planned programme of support. Leaving care workers and social workers tended to take responsibility for co-ordinating services as well as, in some cases, delivering preparation support either on a one-to-one basis or through a training workshop in independent living skills. Other sources of planned preparation support included carers (family, foster and residential staff), voluntary agency staff and specific area-based youth projects. Teachers, health care workers, employment and housing services were also identified as playing a role in planned preparation support, demonstrating a multi-agency approach.

Young people also provided information on who had been involved in generally supporting and preparing them for adult life and how helpful they had been. Table 4.4 illustrates the pattern of responses from the total sample (n=107) and shows that leaving care workers along with parents and foster carers were considered as being most helpful in the preparation process.

How well prepared were young people for leaving care?

The key aim of the throughcare process is to ensure that young people are equipped with the basic skills and abilities (both practical and emotional) necessary for them to make a successful transition to adult life. In order to explore how prepared young people in the study were for moving on from care we collected information on preparation support and life skills from the young people and their main support worker.

Young people were asked whether or not they had received enough information and support prior to them leaving care, in a range of life skills. These included healthy eating, personal care, cooking, cleaning, shopping and budgeting, relationship skills, hobbies, awareness of safe sex practices and issues related to alcohol and drug use. A preparation score based upon these items was calculated with a threshold score to indicate whether a young person was well or less well prepared. Overall, responses indicated

Table 4.4 Who was involved
in preparing young people for adult life?

Who was involved?	% of young people who identified this person	% of young people who felt this person had been		
		very helpful	some help	no help
Parent(s)	87	42	29	29
Social worker	96	26	45	29
Specialist leaving care worker	66	47	24	30
Foster carer	54	40	17	43
Residential worker	53	25	40	35
Teacher	76	32	36	32
Friend(s)	92	32	47	21

that around half (52%) of the sample were well prepared for independent living, while almost half were not. Patterns emerging from further analysis suggested that young people who had spent less time in care (often because they came into care later) and those who left care earlier were less likely than others in the study to be well prepared for independent living.[2] This may be because young people had not had sufficient time or support to learn life skills or because they had left care before embarking upon or completing a programme of preparation support.

There was also some indication that young people were more likely to feel well prepared in particular life skill areas. Analysis showed that most young people felt that they had received enough support in practical living skills (such as cooking and shopping) and health promotion issues (healthy eating, substance misuse and safe sex). Fewer young people, however, felt well prepared with budgeting (with a third reporting having had no information or support) and interpersonal skills, where almost a quarter said they had not had any information or support with relationships.

Support workers were also asked to comment on how prepared they considered young people to be at the point of moving on from care. They were asked to rate young people's skills and abilities across five key life areas. Responses suggested that most young people were reasonably well prepared. Support workers reported that the majority (70%) had good or very good self-care skills and practical skills. Fewer young people, however, were considered to have good interpersonal skills, with over two-fifths (44%) being rated as having poor or very poor skills in this area. A particular area of weakness was young people's self-esteem and confidence. Support workers rated over two-thirds (67%) as being poor or very poor. Furthermore, almost half (47%) of young people were considered to have a poor or very poor sense of self-identity.

These findings suggest that there are particular areas of focus within the preparation process, namely practical living skills (with the exception perhaps of budgeting) and self-care skills (including healthy eating and safe sex). They also indicate that some important areas, such as self-efficacy and self-identity, are more likely to be neglected. Research and practice evidence suggest that young people who have been looked after may experience difficulties with self-esteem and identity resulting from trauma or suffering experienced before they entered care, the impact of care and the likelihood of multiple moves and the stigma attached to care itself (Department of Health 1995). This emphasises the need for a more balanced and holistic approach which pays attention to developing young people's interpersonal and relationship skills and nurturing self-efficacy through raising self-esteem and confidence, alongside the more traditional areas of practical living skills.

How does preparation help?

Good preparation – or throughcare – can provide the foundation stone for a successful transition to adult living (although we should bear in mind that the realities of independent living may challenge even those most able and well prepared). So far, we have provided some indication of how prepared young people in the study felt (and were perceived) as they moved on from care. However, we have not yet explored the effectiveness of preparation support in helping them to adapt to post-care living. One means of measuring the effectiveness of preparation is to consider its impact on young people's ability to cope in certain life skill areas after leaving care. Another is to look at the relationship between preparation and the extent to which young people achieve positive outcomes across a range of life areas. These issues (coping with adult life and outcomes) were assessed at the six-month follow-up stage. The findings, which are discussed in full in Chapter 8, suggest that preparation is indeed associated with young people's coping ability.

Planning for leaving care

This final section will briefly look at leaving care planning. In addition to preparing young people for the time they are no longer looked after, local authorities are also responsible for assisting young people to make a well-planned transition from care. As noted earlier, some young people move on to independent living earlier than anticipated. Crisis, placement breakdown and individual choice mean that some unplanned or unantici-pated moves from care are difficult to avoid. Nevertheless, it is important that young people are assisted to plan what they will do after they leave care. This is often best facilitated through a leaving care review.

Information on planning young people's move from care was collected from support workers in our three case study authorities. It suggested that a formal leaving care review had been held for three-fifths (60%) of young people in the sample. On average the review took place just seven weeks prior to them leaving care.

Leaving care reviews provide an opportunity for support workers, young people themselves and other relevant parties to identify specific needs and issues through a needs assessment. Workers were asked to identify the main areas in which an assessment of need had been made for young people during the leaving care planning and review process. Infor-mation demonstrated the emphasis placed on traditional areas of support, such as accommodation and education and employment (addressed in 75% and 88% of cases respectively). In over half of cases, future sources of pro-fessional support (68%), informal support networks (65%), financial skills (61%) and life skills (51%) had been addressed. However, less than half of these young people had been assessed in terms of welfare benefits (43%), health needs (38%) and leisure and hobbies (27%).

We also asked young people who had helped them to plan what they would do after leaving care. Almost half of the young people in the sample acknowledged the role of leaving care workers and social workers in the planning process, while over a quarter (27%) identified residential staff and 17 per cent reported help from foster carers. Other sources of help included friends and partners, voluntary agency staff, homeless person's officers and the church.

Conclusion

This chapter has focused on the process of preparing young people for leaving care and moving on to independent living. It has considered this process (known as throughcare) in terms of wider local authority policy and procedures for providing support as well as how it was delivered and experienced in practice in the three local authority areas.

Information from the national policy survey of all local authorities showed that the throughcare service was patchy and variable across Scotland, with some areas operating their own eligibility criteria.

The case study of three Scottish local authorities confirmed some of these findings. It also demonstrated some of the challenges for policy makers and throughcare practitioners as they develop and deliver preparation support to young people leaving care.

For example, we have seen that the majority of young people in our study had not received a planned programme of preparation support. An examination of the reasons for this highlighted a number of key challenges facing throughcare services in providing structured support to prepare young people for independent living. They suggested the need for a well-planned, well-timed and inclusive programme of support and highlighted the difficulties of engaging some young people in a structured preparation programme.

We have also seen that a wide range of people were instrumental in helping young people to prepare and plan for post-care living, whether on a formal or informal basis. Sources of support ranged from specialist leaving care workers, social workers, family and carers to teachers, health care workers and voluntary agency staff, thus demonstrating a collaborative approach.

Importantly, this chapter has explored young people's preparedness for leaving care, from their own perspective as well as that of their support worker. We have seen that while most young people felt well prepared in practical and self-care skills, they felt less able in budgeting and managing relationships. There was further evidence from support workers that interpersonal skills and self-esteem and confidence were areas of weakness for many young people as they moved on from care.

Finally, we have explored the process of planning young people's move from care. Findings showed that less than half of young people in the study had received a leaving care review, although for those who had, many had received a needs assessment in most key life areas. Again, however, it was possible to identify certain areas that appeared to be of lower priority, such as health-care needs and hobbies.

Having looked at preparation and planning, we will next focus on young people's experience of moving on from care and their initial post-care outcomes.

Notes

1 The *Looking After Children* (LAC) materials, which were developed in England, aim to improve the recording, assessing, planning and reviews process regarding children who are looked after away from home. They were adapted and introduced in Scotland in 1997.

2 This finding, however, was not statistically significant at the p=0.05 level. A Mann Whitney test to measure the relationship between the young person's preparedness and both the number of months in care during the last/only care episode and the age at which they left were p=0.06 and p=0.07 respectively.

Chapter 5

Moving On From Care:
The Leaving Care Experience and
Early Post-care Destinations

I like the way things went, I think things moved smooth from moving from my foster parents to here [supported lodgings]. I'm happy with the amount of support I got, my link worker has been the most [help], and my landlady. Now and again if I can't get the advice from them my foster family are always there. (Lucy)

From the age of seven I always dreamed of being 16 so that I could leave care. I never thought it would be like this. (Brian)

Introduction

Leaving care is a significant event for most young people who have been looked after. However, too often, it is identified with the age of leaving, as shown by Brian above. Ideally, it should be a process involving being prepared and supported for adult living, making the transition from care, and receiving ongoing support to cope with life after care (Pinkerton and McCrea 1999).

This chapter focuses on making the transition from care. It looks at the experience of moving on from care for young people from our three local authorities. In the first part of the chapter, we explore the actual process of leaving care in terms of when and how it occurred. In the second part of the chapter, we discuss the initial destinations and outcomes for young people during the early months of post-care living. This involves a descriptive account of what young people were doing and how they were coping. We look at their early housing and career paths, their health and well-being, any difficulties they experienced and any factors which helped them to make progress.

Young people's experiences of leaving care

Leaving care can cover a range of situations. For some young people it will involve a move to independent living, either before or after their supervision requirement has ended. For others, it will involve a return home to family, while some young people will remain at home with parents or remain with foster carers after their supervision requirement has been discharged. We have tried to capture the full range of experiences as we explore and describe the transition from care to post-care living.

Most young people leave care far earlier than other young people leave home, often before they are 18 years of age. Explanations for this pattern are many and varied. Certainly, for most young people who are looked after, approaching the age of 16 signifies a turning point in their lives. Not only are they able to leave school but many young people see it as their first opportunity to move on to independent living and will do so whether or not they are otherwise prepared.

In recent years, however, the prevailing culture has been to reverse this trend by delaying young people's move from care until after their 18th birthday. One of the main aims of the Children (Leaving Care) Act, introduced in England and Wales in October 2001, was to prevent unplanned, unprepared and, where possible, early moves from care to independent living.[1]

Indications from this study suggest that, to date, progress has been relatively slow. Information on the age at which young people had left care or moved onto independent living showed that almost three-quarters (73%) of young people had left care at 15 or 16 years of age – less than a tenth (6%) had remained in care after their 18th birthday. The average age for young people leaving care in our study was 16 years.

Analysis was carried out to see whether there were any patterns which may help explain why some young people leave care earlier than others.

We found no significant difference in the age at which males and females in the study had left care; however, an area analysis identified some patterns in the age of leaving care across the three local authorities. For example, almost all (92%) of the young people leaving care in County had done so at 15 or 16 years of age compared to 66 per cent of those from City and 64 per cent of those from Shire (p=0.022). Indeed, the average age of young people leaving care in County was 15.8 years, compared to 16.2 and 16.3 years of age for Shire and City.

We were aware that some young people who had become looked after because of school non-attendance were likely to have come off their supervision requirement when they left school (15.5 years old being the first point at which they were able). Many of those looked after for this reason had remained at home with parents on a home supervision requirement and, as we know, almost a third (30%) of young people in our sample had been looked after at home. There was a chance, therefore, that this group may have skewed (or distorted) the general picture. Analysis was carried out to see whether this group had in fact influenced the overall pattern of responses. However, we found no evidence to suggest that this was the case for our sample.

We also looked at where young people had been looked after prior to leaving care. This enabled us to test whether there was any difference in the age at which young people left care from different placement types.

We found some association between the average age at which young people moved on from care and where they had moved on from (p=0.015). For example, those young people who had been looked after at home tended to leave care (i.e. have their supervision requirement discharged) at an earlier age (16 years on average) than young people placed away from home in residential care or foster care (16.5 and 17 years respectively). Overall, those placed in foster care appeared to remain in their care placements longer compared to young people from other placement types, including residential schools, secure units and other relatives. In fact, all those who had left care aged 18 or over had been looked after in foster care (p=0.005).

A further factor associated with the age at which young people left care was the age at which they had entered care. Analysis of young people's last care episode suggested that those who had entered care early (aged 13 or under) were more likely to leave care later. In fact, young people who had come into care before the age of 14 were twice as likely to stay in care beyond their 17th birthday as those who entered care at 14 or over (46% and 21% respectively, p=0.036).

Moving to independent living

As outlined at the beginning of this section, not all young people who leave care will move straight onto independent living. Just over a tenth (13%) of young people in our study had returned home after leaving care and almost a quarter (24%) had remained with parents when their home supervision requirement ended. Around half (52%), however, did go on to independent living.[2]

Consistent within previous UK research, the majority (89%) of those who had moved to independent living had done so before the age of 18. This contrasts starkly with figures reported in a recent study of Scottish young people, which showed that 94 per cent of males and 88 per cent of females were still living in the parental home at 18 (Furlong *et al.* 2003).

Moving on from care to independent living at the early age of 16 is a concern. However, for some young people an early move from care can represent a positive step on the pathway to independence. For example, a move to supported carers can provide an important breathing space where young people can develop their skills and confidence before embarking upon fully independent living. What is of equal importance, therefore, is that young people are able to leave care in a planned and supported manner, and, as we shall discuss in the following section, that they are able to have a say in when they leave.

Reasons for leaving care

Young people who had been looked after away from home were asked whether they felt that they had a choice about when they left their care placement. Only a third (33%) felt that they had chosen when to leave although 26 per cent said they had 'some choice' in the matter. Two in five (40%) young people, however, said that they had not had a choice.

Reasons for leaving care were varied, although it was possible to identify some common themes. Not surprisingly, age was significant for many. Some, like Sally, felt that it signalled the right opportunity to take responsibility for their life: 'I left care because I was 16, I felt ready and wanted to move on and become independent.' Others felt that they had outgrown the provision and facilities provided through the care system. Steven, for example, had left care at 16 to live with friends. He told us, 'I left [care] coz I was out of place, one of the oldest in the residential school.' A similar situation arose for Ivan, who was 17 when he left residential care: 'I was older than all the other residents and staff thought it was time for me to move on. I agreed because I was getting fed up with being in a home with younger kids.' At 17, Frank also felt he had outgrown his care placement. He told us, 'I was too old for care and the foster parents had new kids.'

There was also evidence that conflict between young people and their carers – over what were perceived as 'unfair rules and regulations' – could precipitate a move from care. Tilly left her foster placement at 16 to move into her own tenancy. She told us: 'I had turned 16 and none of the rules had changed, like the time to be in…this led to arguments until the point I felt unwanted and chose it would be best for everyone if I moved out.'

Placement breakdown due to behaviour problems or crisis was also a reason for leaving care. Some young people, however, felt 'pushed out' of their care placement. Tom, who left his children's home at 15 to move into a hostel, said, 'I got told I was leaving.' This was also the case for Angie who had returned home temporarily at 16 while waiting for alternative accommodation. She told us she 'had to leave the residential school because they didn't want the responsibility of me falling pregnant in their care'.

Finally, for some young people, the decision to leave care had coincided with other life changes, such as going to college or university, having a child or setting up home with a partner.

Early post-care destinations

Having looked at young people's experiences of leaving care, this section follows them into the early months of post-care living. As the quotes at the opening of the chapter suggest, young people have very different experiences of moving on from care. While some will have a positive journey, others may find that the reality of leaving care may not always match their expectations. This section of the chapter explores the initial destinations of all young people who took part in the study. Information was collected at the point at which young people joined the study (baseline) and provides an insight into their circumstances and experiences, including where they were living, their career status and their general health and well-being in the early months after leaving care. We start by looking at their early career paths.

Early career paths

For some care leavers, the legacy of poor schooling and low educational attainment is evident in their subsequent career paths. While educational disadvantage casts a long shadow for any young person, previous research documents the increased likelihood of unemployment and dependency on welfare benefits amongst the care leaver group. The analysis of data from the National Child Development Study UK revealed that young people leaving care were much more likely to be unemployed or be in unskilled or semi-skilled work, and were less likely to be in managerial work, than their non-care peers (Cheung and Heath 1994). Similarly, a survey of leaving care projects working with 2905 care leavers showed that 51 per cent were unemployed – two and a half times the unemployment rate for the age range in general (Broad 1998). More recent figures produced by the Scottish Executive also highlight the gap in participation rates between care leavers and their non-care peers. They show that around 60 per cent of care leavers were not in education, employment or training (a status commonly referred to by the acronym NEET) compared to 14 per cent of all 16- to19-year-olds in Scotland (Scottish Executive 2003).

Data from our own study enabled us to focus on young people's career status at the point of entering the study (an average of six months after moving on from care). This involved exploring patterns of participation in post-compulsory education, training and work and considering the incidence of non-participation for this group of 15- to 20-year-olds.

Information from young people suggested that almost two in five (39%) were engaged in education, training or work in the early months after leaving care. This included a small proportion (3%) who had undertaken voluntary work. Of those who had embarked upon a career path, slightly more young men appeared to be engaged in paid work while those in education were more likely to be young women. In addition to participation in full-time employment and further education courses, there was some evidence of casual work (part-time bar work, washing dishes and appointments through temping agencies) and short-term education and training courses (basic skills and literacy workshops and taster courses).

Around three in five young people (61%), however, were not in education, employment or training (NEET). This group included young people who were unemployed and a small number of young women whose main activity was caring for their child. Table 5.1 indicates the pattern of responses across the main career status groups. The findings from the study are broadly comparable to recent national figures for Scottish care leavers, which show that around a quarter were in employment or training (Scottish Executive 2003).

Table 5.1 Career status of young people at baseline

Occupation status	% of young people (n=103)
Voluntary work	3
Caring for child	4
Training	11
Employed	11
Education	14
Unemployed	57

The pattern of non-participation remained fairly consistent across the three research authorities with around half of young people in County and City and over two-thirds (68%) of young people in Shire being unemployed.

Also, there did not appear to be any relationship between non-participation and a young person's educational attainment while at school. A possible explanation is that some young people had entered education after leaving care to make up for poor educational attainment. However, there was some indication that truancy may be related to non-participation after care. Analysis showed that young people who had often truanted while at school were more likely to be in the NEET group than young people who had never truanted (p=0.035).

While the overall picture from the study reveals a tendency towards non-participation in education, training and work, this cannot be disconnected from some wider social trends affecting young people in general. Many studies have highlighted the changing nature of the youth labour market over the past two decades and the difficulties faced by young people generally as they attempt to enter employment. The decline in traditional industry, rising demand for an educated and specialised workforce and the increase in temporary or part-time employment have resulted in limited career opportunities and make it financially difficult for many young people to live independently. Studies of youth transitions have also highlighted the trend within the general population for young people to delay entry to the workforce. An increasing number decide instead on the growing amount of 'transitional' options, such as further and higher education, vocational training courses, apprenticeships and other work-based learning initiatives.

However, in addition to issues facing young people in general, those leaving care may face further obstacles to participating in education, employment or training. Some may not have the opportunity to use informal networks as a source of finding work or support to sustain participation. Furthermore, the need to find a level of employment or income that will provide them with the means to facilitate and sustain their early transition to independent living may prove a disincentive for many. Some may also face barriers to pursuing education and training options either through personal circumstances, lack of qualifications or limited financial resources. Indeed, recent research into care leavers in higher education has highlighted the lack of financial, practical and emotional support for those attending university. Difficulties in meeting their education and living costs, having nowhere to return to during vacation, and mounting debts have been documented. Against this background, it perhaps is unsurprising to find that only 1 per cent of looked after young people enter higher education (Jackson *et al.* 2003).

This snapshot of young people's career outcomes in the initial months of post-care living gives some indication of the difficulties they face in finding a foothold on the career ladder. Further information on changes and progress within career outcomes over time was gathered from young people who took part in the six-month follow-up study and is discussed in Chapter 8.

Income

For young people in the general population the extended transition from school to work and independent living may be cushioned by the financial support of the family. For young people moving on from care, such support systems are not always in place. Furthermore, as we have already discussed, care leavers tend to embark on this transition far sooner than their non-care peers and the impact of poor educational and employment outcomes can leave many ill-prepared for an increasingly competitive youth labour market. Barriers to employment and changes to the benefits system in recent years that have affected all young people have served to increase the risk of financial hardship amongst this group. It is, therefore, perhaps unsurprising that UK studies completed since the mid-1970s have consistently shown that the vast majority of care leavers live at or near the poverty line (Broad 1999; Pinkerton and McCrea 1999; Stein 1997).

It was apparent that financial hardship was an issue for young people in our own study. Young people were asked to state how much money they had to live on each week. Many (59%) told us that they survived on less than £35 a week, an amount below the standard benefits level. Just over a third (35%) received between £39 and £80 and a small proportion (6%) had a weekly income above £80. The average weekly income for the group as a whole was £65.16; however, around a tenth (11%) of young people reported that they had no income at all.

The main source of income within the group was benefits, with 42 per cent of young people claiming income support or Jobseekers Allowance.[3] A wage provided the main source of income for 13 per cent, and varied from £10 for a young woman who received an allowance for her voluntary work to £120 for a young woman in full-time employment. Education grants and training allowances accounted for 4 per cent and 10 per cent respectively, and 5 per cent of the group relied on payments from the social work department. There was also evidence that some young people, particularly those without more formal sources of income, relied on money from parents, babysitting jobs, bridging or crisis loans and, in the case of one young person, the proceeds of selling drugs.

It was evident that many young people had experienced financial problems. Around eight in ten (85%) said they had been short of money at some point since leaving care and over a quarter (28%) said that this was always the case. Debt was also an issue and over a third (35%) reported

having debts that they were unable to pay off. These debts included catalogue payments, fines and loans. Some young people had been able to turn
to parents and relatives for help. One young woman told us, 'Mum paid off
the crisis loan and catalogue money; she tries to show me how to budget my
money so it will last until I next get paid.' Social services and voluntary
agencies were also sources of support in a crisis. Craig told us, '[A voluntary
worker] continuously helps since I have difficulty in managing money and
I'm awaiting supplementation from social work till my benefits kick in.'

FINANCIAL ASSISTANCE
Financial assistance from social services was available to care leavers under
Sections 29 and 30 of the Children (Scotland) Act 1995. Information
provided by support workers suggested that around 50 per cent of young
people had received financial assistance in the early months of leaving care.
Payments made to young people under Sections 29 and 30 included a range
of support. A third had received a leaving care grant for setting up home.
Amounts ranged from £300 to £1700, depending on the young person's
circumstances. Almost half (46%) had received accommodation subsidies,
most on a regular basis, and a third had received income top-ups, either on a
one-off or regular basis. Social services had also assisted some young people
(9%) to pay off debts.

In terms of mainstream financial assistance, there was some evidence
that young people had experienced difficulties in accessing financial
support through the benefits system. Problems included difficulties in
getting and completing the relevant application forms and delays in
payments, particularly where young people's circumstances were often
changing. One young person told us, 'the benefits advisor made me wait
three weeks for a decision'. Overall, however, around two-fifths (42%) of
those who had been in contact with the Benefits Agency had found them
helpful. Arianne was on income support and claiming housing benefit; she
had been happy with the service and advice from the benefits advisor: 'Benefits told me what to apply for and told me what was available; they sorted
out money for me to live on.'

Accommodation

A key issue for young people moving on from care, and indeed leaving care
policy, is where they live. The Social Justice Milestones for tackling social
exclusion state that all young people leaving local authority care 'should
have access to appropriate housing options'. They also state that 'no-one has
to sleep rough' (Scottish Executive 1999).

As we have seen, in comparison to young people in the general population, young people who have been looked after tend to move to independent living sooner, may be more likely to be without family support and the option for return home, and have less choice about the timing and nature of the move. Also, many struggle financially and subsequently may find it difficult to keep up the costs of running a home. Previous research evidence also suggests that these young people are likely to experience insecure housing careers and transitory accommodation and are over-represented in the homeless population (Biehal *et al.* 1995; Randall 1988, 1989; Stein *et al.* 2000).

This section provides an overview of the housing situation of all young people in the study. While it is recognised that housing opportunities are ultimately determined by wider factors, such as local housing provision and local authority housing policies and availability, we have drawn upon individual circumstances to explore accommodation options as well as the processes involved in housing mobility. We have used this section to explore the type of accommodation young people were living in within the early months after leaving care, their ability to manage and sustain their accommodation and any initial difficulties they faced.

At the point of entering the study almost two-fifths (37%) of young people between the ages of 15 and 20 were living at home with one or both parents. Most of these had been looked after within the parental home on a home supervision requirement.

The majority (52%) of young people in the study were living in independent or semi-independent accommodation, the most common being supported lodgings and hostels (13% in each). Around one in ten were living alone in their own tenancy and 14 per cent were evenly distributed amongst friends, foster/support carers and living with a partner. A small proportion (5%) were living with other relatives, such as grandparents, aunts and siblings, while a similar number were staying in transitory accommodation, such as bed and breakfasts, a rough sleepers hostel and staying with a boyfriend's parents.

An area analysis showed that young people from Shire were far more likely to be living in their own tenancy (either alone or with a partner) than young people from County and City (41% of young people from Shire compared to 10% from City and 7% from County; p=0.006). The most common types of accommodation (other than family home) were supported lodgings in County (15% of young people) and hostels in City (17% of young people).

MOVING

Some degree of housing movement is normal for young adults and may be brought about by positive influences, such as finding a job, going to college, moving nearer to family or setting up home with a partner. For young people in the wider population, housing mobility generally progresses towards better quality and more secure accommodation during their early housing careers (Jones 1987). However, movement brought about by negative reasons, such as crisis, debt or inability to manage, may result in less positive outcomes.

Previous research has suggested that young people who have been looked after tend to experience a high rate of movement. In *Moving On* (Biehal *et al.* 1995) nearly a third of the sample had at least two additional moves within a few months of leaving care.

In our study, information on housing mobility was gathered mainly from young people who had taken part in the follow-up study. Young people were asked how many times they had moved accommodation since leaving care, an average of 12 months earlier. Responses indicated that almost two-thirds (61%) had experienced at least one accommodation move since moving on from care. The average number of accommodation moves (subsequent to the initial move from care) for those that had moved was four. The majority (61%) had moved home on three or more occasions.

Those who reported several accommodation moves tended to have experienced insecure and transitory accommodation types, such as living with friends, returning to unsatisfactory family accommodation through necessity or staying in hostels or bed and breakfasts. An indication of housing mobility is provided by Adam, who summarised his experience of independent living over the 12 months since leaving care:

> I left foster care because I was 16 years old [and] went to live with [a friend]. I then presented as homeless and lived in a B & B 'til I got thrown out and went to live with my dad. I got thrown out and went to live with my mum 'til I got thrown out for giving cheek. I went to live with my sister [but] I was asked to leave there for fighting with her boyfriend. I then went back and presented as homeless and was put in a B & B 'til [support worker] helped me find supported lodgings.

Brian, meanwhile, told us that he had moved ten times in ten months, mostly moving from one hostel or homeless unit to the next and intermittently returning to his mum.

Reasons for movement were varied. The most common issues precipitating a move were a breakdown in relationship with family, friends or carers. Gill had lost count of the number of moves she had made since leaving the residential unit eight months previously:

> I moved back to mum's, things didn't work out, she still treated me like I was a wee lassie. From friends to homeless accommodation eight or nine times, the arrangements kept breaking down. [Now] living with boyfriend but not getting on so well and the accommodation is not secure. The council don't know I'm living here and my boyfriend is afraid he'll get chucked out…I'm going to have to go back to homeless accommodation.

Some young people talked of being evicted or being asked to leave their accommodation. Carol told us, 'I got chucked out of my first house. I also got chucked out of my mum's. [I] stayed with friends then moved back to mum's then I was in a homeless unit for about three weeks.' Amanda, who had been living with support carers, was also asked to leave. 'I was put out of the carers when I told her I was pregnant. I had nowhere to go and felt I must have done something wrong.'

Crisis moves brought about by intimidation from other residents, fleeing violence, or an unsafe area were also amongst young people's reasons for moving accommodation. Rachel moved out of her tenancy after a few months. She told us, 'I'm staying with mum at the moment because I can't stay at my own flat because it isn't safe.'

Some young people moved to improve their living conditions whether towards more stability, a better or safer area or a better standard of accommodation. Craig had moved three times since leaving care. His experience highlights the difficulties of living in poor or problem housing. '[First] I moved coz of neighbours and then I went to a private rent with my girlfriend. The state of the house and dodgy landlord made us move again.'

Two issues that particularly stood out amongst the reasons for moving were the frequency with which a move home to family (either from care or intermittently during the young person's housing career) broke down and also, as discussed in the next section, the incidence of homelessness.

HOMELESSNESS

Homelessness is a risk amongst young people generally. The Scottish Council for Single Homeless reported that 35 per cent of those presenting as homeless to local authorities were aged under 25 (Scottish Executive 2000a). Difficulties in accessing and sustaining accommodation are driven by the rising costs of housing and higher education, a competitive youth labour market and limited social housing availability. For more vulnerable young people, these difficulties can be compounded by fractured family or support networks, emotional, mental or physical health problems or substance misuse. These issues suggest that some care-experienced young people may be at particular risk of housing crisis.

Young people in the study were asked if they had been homeless since leaving care. Almost two-fifths (38%) reported that they had experienced homelessness either currently or since leaving care. All of these young people were under 20 years of age. Our findings also suggested that homelessness was not just a problem in large cities. Over twice as many young people from Shire authority appeared to have experienced homelessness, when compared to County and City young people (65% compared to 33% and 29% respectively).

For most young people homelessness had involved staying with friends or in homeless hostels or units. Few mentioned sleeping rough. Josh from City, who had moved nine times and had been homeless on several occasions, said, 'I was fortunate really not to be sleeping rough. I always had a kip on somebody's floor though it wasn't exactly the Ritz or nothing.'

DIFFICULTIES WITH ACCOMMODATION

Despite the extent of homelessness and housing movement, most young people said they were happy with their accommodation arrangements at the point of entering the study. However, just over a quarter (27%) reported problems. The types of problems young people described tended to fall into accommodation-specific categories. For example, young people living at home described having difficulties with parents or siblings. Brian had returned home after leaving residential school. He told us that things were not working out at home. 'It's my parents' drinking and brother's drug habit. My life's not good…[it] would be better if I could have my own flat. That's all I want.' More commonly, young people told us about arguments with parents or having to re-adjust to family life, as in Jessica's case. 'I'm not happy here as I've not lived with mum since I was 13, I only visited.'

Those living in their own tenancies, meanwhile, were more likely to describe feeling lonely or isolated. Deb had moved from a residential school into her own flat at 17. She told us, 'It's really difficult when you leave a school that's full of lassies and go and live by yourself. I still find it difficult.' Also for Heather from County, who was otherwise coping well in her own tenancy, the difficulties were 'being away from my mum, I'm only 16 and still a bairn and get a bit weepy at times'.

Feeling unsafe, either within the accommodation or the area in which it was located, was also an issue for some young people. Anna had recently moved in to her own tenancy with her partner and their baby but was trying to get re-housed. 'Local gangs were causing problems to us in the middle of the night when we first moved in, kicking our door, hammering on windows. By the time the police arrived they'd moved on.'

As noted earlier, however, many young people were generally happy with their accommodation and reported positive experiences. Barry, who had moved in with friends after leaving care at 16, told us, 'I get on with the people I'm living with. I do some babysitting for them. I'm treated like one of the family.' This was also the case for Lynn, a young woman living with support carers:

> Usually if things go bad then I'm the kind of person who wants to move on. But when things go bad here as it does everywhere, I want to talk it through and get it sorted right away…I know that even if things are bad I still love them and I want to be here, no matter what.

Some young people felt that being happy and settled in their accommodation had a positive impact on other areas of their life. For example, Carrie had lived at home with her parents after leaving care but had left when relationships broke down. After a period of homelessness and living in bed and breakfasts Carrie finally moved into her own tenancy. She felt that moving things had gone well since, and told us, 'I feel more relaxed, more good tempered. I enjoy my own space and have a better relationship with mum now that I have left home.'

Meeting the accommodation needs of young people leaving care is an important factor is helping them to make a successful transition to independent adult living. A settled and safe living environment is often seen as one of the foundation stones on which to build a positive career path and, as the quote above demonstrates, aid family and social networks. We will return to the important issue of accommodation in Chapter 8 when we explore, in more detail, the housing outcomes of those who took part in the six-month follow-up study.

Health, well-being and difficulties

Some young people who have been looked after will have particular needs over and above those of other looked after young people. These needs may be related to a disability, physical or mental health difficulty, learning difficulties or problems with drugs, alcohol or offending and should be identified and addressed as part of the throughcare and aftercare process (Broad 2005).

This final section focuses on the health and general well-being needs of young people moving on from care. It also explores negative lifestyle issues, such as difficulties with substance misuse and offending. Information in this section is drawn from the accounts of young people and their support workers and includes information gathered from those who took part in the six-month follow-up study. We have also drawn on existing research evidence to highlight some key issues.

DISABILITY AND MENTAL AND PHYSICAL HEALTH DIFFICULTIES

Research evidence indicates that young disabled people have a greater like-lihood of being in care than other young people. Gordon *et al.*'s re-analysis of the Office of Population, Census and Surveys' (OPCS) disability survey found that 6 per cent of children with disabilities in England and Wales were in care compared with 0.5 per cent of the under-18 population as a whole. Furthermore, recent UK research into young disabled people leaving care suggests that a quarter of care leavers may be disabled in some way and that many are denied suitable housing options and appropriate and timely support packages to facilitate independent living (Rabiee and Priestley 2001).

Research also suggests that young people who have been looked after are likely to have a greater vulnerability to learning difficulties, emotional and behavioural difficulties and mental health issues. Indeed, as Koprowska and Stein (2000) point out, some of these issues may have been brought about by the experiences and conditions that led to the young person entering care. The incidence of mental health difficulties amongst young people with a care background has been highlighted in several studies. McCann *et al.* (1996) found that over half (57%) of young people in foster care and nearly all (96%) of young people in residential care had some form of psychiatric disorder. A more recent study found that 45 per cent of looked after children aged between 5 and 17 were assessed as having a mental health problem (Meltzer *et al.* 2003) and findings from the Scottish Health Feedback Survey (2001/2002) indicated that 45 per cent of care-experienced young people had self-harmed and many showed signs of depression and low self-esteem.

To date there has been a little research into the physical health of care-experienced young people. However, a recent survey which focused on the overall health of care leavers in Scotland found that young people consid-ered leaving care to have had a negative impact on their health and reported that many displayed health risk behaviours, such as substance misuse, smoking, poor diet and lack of physical exercise (Scottish Health Feedback Survey 2002). More general studies of the care leaver population suggest the need for greater policy and practice attention on general health educa-tion. This includes promoting healthy lifestyles through support and infor-mation to address diet, leisure, safe sex and risk behaviours, in addition to monitoring identified health problems and carrying out in-care health checks and needs assessments on leaving care (Biehal *et al.* 1995; Broad 1999, 2003; Stein and Wade 2000).

There is also evidence that young people leaving care with specific needs (whether a disability, or physical or mental health difficulties) may face increased disadvantage as they attempt to embark upon independent living. Studies have shown that young disabled people and those with learning difficulties are over-represented amongst those not participating in education and training and that economic activity is significantly lower amongst this group (Tomlinson 1996). Previous research has also suggested that those with mental health problems are at greater risk of poverty, poor housing, social isolation and unemployment (Buchanan 1999; Meltzer *et al.* 2002).

Despite clear evidence of need, there have been concerns that the health and well-being needs of young people in and leaving care have in the past been neglected both in policy and practice. A study of the health needs of looked after young people in Edinburgh, for example, found major gaps in knowledge about young people's health (Robson *et al.* 1999) and a more recent health survey carried out in Glasgow reported that young people looked after in and leaving local authority care were particularly vulnerable to systemic and personal barriers to good health (Scottish Health Feedback Survey 2002). Findings from our own policy survey also suggested that the health needs of care leavers was a lower priority for local authorities nationally, but one that was increasingly recognised as needing more attention (Dixon and Stein 2002b).

Information on the health needs of young people in our study was gathered from young people and their support workers. Many (47%) young people said they felt well and had no health problems. However, as shown in Table 5.2, over a tenth (12%) reported having a long-term physical health problem, while almost a fifth (19%) reported having other health problems, such as asthma, eczema, hearing impairments or problems associated with drug or alcohol misuse.

A relatively small proportion (6%) of young people reported having a mental health problem. This included depression, agoraphobia, eating disorders and self-harming. It is possible, however, that the extent to which these difficulties were present in the group is more accurately reflected in the information provided by support workers. Assessments from workers suggested that 41 per cent of young people had emotional or behavioural difficulties. This included depression, eating disorders, verbal, physical or sexual aggression, threatening or volatile behaviour, alcoholism, offending, mood swings, ADHD, self-harm and emotional issues related to past experiences of abuse, bereavement or rejection.

Table 5.2 Young people's reports of disability and health needs

	% of young people
Disability	5
Mental health problem	6
Physical health problem	12
Other health problems	19
Learning difficulties	31

SUPPORT WITH HEALTH NEEDS

The Children (Scotland) Act 1995 Regulations and Guidance emphasises the role of local authorities in considering the specific needs of young people in and leaving care and identifying the necessary services and resources for meeting these needs. Health needs had been assessed during the leaving care planning and review process for a quarter of young people taking part in the study. In 8 per cent of cases, the need for specialist therapeutic services had been identified.

In terms of health promotion issues, it appeared that most young people felt that they had received enough information and support with issues, such as safe sex (64%) and the risks associated with substance misuse (72%) and smoking (66%). Slightly fewer felt that they had received sufficient support with healthy eating (56%) and keeping fit (52%).

It was also evident that the majority of young people had access to mainstream health services after leaving care. Most (84%) told us they were registered with a GP and 62 per cent were registered with a dentist, although up to a fifth (18%) were unsure whether they were registered with either. In a small number of cases young people mentioned support from specialist services, such as mental health workers or drug and alcohol services. Generally, however, young people tended to comment on more generic sources of support with health and well-being needs, such as help from GPs, social workers and leaving care staff. For example, almost all those who reported having mental health problems identified help from their social worker or leaving care worker rather than a mental health worker. Some young people also described the support they had received from family, friends, residential staff and foster carers. In most cases this involved help with setting up or being accompanied to GP and hospital appointments and encouragement to seek help.

DIFFICULTIES WITH SUBSTANCE MISUSE AND OFFENDING

Closely related to health and well-being is the issue of substance misuse. Recent statistics suggest that experimenting with drugs and alcohol is increasingly common amongst teenagers in general. The Scottish Crime Survey showed that over a quarter of young people aged between 16 and 19 years of age had tried drugs and almost half of males aged 20 to 24 had done so (Scottish Executive Central Research Unit 2000). Studies also suggest that pre-teen drug use is increasing. Research shows that in some parts of Scotland around 10 per cent of 10- to 12-year-olds have started to use illegal drugs (McKeganey and Norrie 1999). Teenage drinking is also a growing concern. Studies suggest that around a fifth of 12- to 15-year-olds use alcohol (National Centre for Social Research 2000) and the 16–24 age group is the most likely to drink in excess of the recommended weekly limit (MacAskill *et al.* 2001).

There is some evidence that care-experienced young people are at higher risk of substance misuse. A recent study of drug and alcohol use within the care population found higher levels of reported drug use compared with the general population. Around 73 per cent of young people leaving care reported using cannabis and around 10 per cent reported weekly use of a class A drug. In addition, a third reported drinking alcohol at least once a week (Ward *et al.* 2003).

In our study of Scottish care leavers, just under a quarter (22%) reported problems with substance misuse, either since leaving care or in the past, with 14 per cent reporting problems with alcohol and 15 per cent having experienced problems with drug use. Some had problems with both. Information was also sought from support workers but many did not know whether the young person they were working with had problems associated with substance misuse. Information from support workers was, therefore, only provided for 49 cases (under half of the total study sample); however, it revealed that over a quarter (29%) of these young people were considered to have moderate to serious problems with substance misuse.

Of those young people who reported having had substance misuse difficulties, just under half (41%) said they had received support to address their problems. Several mentioned support from specialist drug and alcohol services and one young person had received help with drugs from her mental health worker. In some cases young people relied on leaving care staff and informal sources of support. One young woman told us, 'I used to have problems with both [drugs and alcohol] but the people from the church I had just joined were very helpful to me.' Young people also talked about receiving leaflets and information from leaving care services. One young man who had problems with drugs said, 'My social worker used to do quiz sheets with me about its effects, then they referred me to a detox unit.'

In addition to asking about drug use, we also explored the extent to which offending was evident amongst the group. Over a quarter (28%) of young people reported having been convicted of a criminal offence in the past 12 months. Offences included burglary, fighting and shoplifting. A tenth of these young people were described as persistent offenders by their support worker. One young person described how he had stolen for an 'associate' in return for accommodation, and another told us he made a living from selling drugs. Just under a tenth (7%) had become looked after because of offending and at least two young people had received a custodial sentence since leaving care. Males in the survey were three times more likely than females to have been convicted of an offence (21% compared to 9%; p=0.005). We were told by several of those young people who had problems with offending that they were attempting to steer clear of crime. One young man highlighted the importance of a stable lifestyle for staying out of trouble. 'Causing trouble and being in jail – that's in the past. I just hope I will stay out of trouble a bit longer by getting a proper job and my own home.'

Of those who had been convicted of a criminal offence since leaving care all had received some form of support. Most mentioned the help of solicitors and the practical support they had received from support workers who had accompanied them to court, explained procedures or provided transport to and from hearings or meetings with solicitors. One young woman who had received help with anger management from her leaving care worker told us, 'They helped me. I've not committed any offences for almost nine months.'

Finally, there was evidence that such difficulties could be accumulative and have an impact upon wider life areas. Some of the more vulnerable young people within the group tended to be at risk of multiple difficulties. For example, around a quarter (26%) of young people had two or more difficulties, some who had difficulties with substance misuse also had problems with other forms of offending and 5 per cent of those with substance misuse problems also had difficulties with mental health or emotional and behavioural difficulties as well as offending. Furthermore, as we see later in Chapter 8, those with difficulties were at greater risk of problems such as poor life skills and post-care instability, such as unemployment or housing mobility.

Conclusion

This chapter has looked at the experience of moving on from care and the early months of post-care living. In doing so it has highlighted some of the challenges facing young people, and those who support them, as they make the transition from care to adult living.

We have explored issues associated with the age at which young people left care, on average at 16 years old, and the factors that influenced their choice and reasons for how and when they moved on. We have also looked at the initial destinations of the group. While many were doing well, some were experiencing considerable difficulties.

These patterns within the data suggests that there are certain indicators which may help us to identify which groups of young people are more likely to leave care early and thus enable support workers to deliver more timely and targeted support to help delay premature transitions to assist and plan supported moves. As we have seen, young people who enter care later and those looked after at home or in residential care appeared to leave care earlier than those in foster care. There was also some evidence that the age at which young people had left care varied across different local authorities and was a key influence generally in how and when a young person moved on from care. Further issues included the availability of age-appropriate care placements as well as post-care accommodation and choice.

Two in five young people had embarked upon a career path within the early months of leaving care; however, there was evidence of difficulties in finding employment, training and education for most. Also, despite a range of support from leaving care services, there was evidence of the financial difficulties young people encountered in meeting the responsibilities of independent living. More than half reported surviving on a weekly allowance below the benefits level and many reported problems with debt.

We also looked at the initial housing situation of those leaving care, in terms of both the various options available and housing mobility and homelessness. The extent to which young people in the group had experienced housing breakdown (38% had been homeless) and movement (61% had moved three or more times since leaving care) introduced the importance of being well prepared and supported for coping with independent living – an issue which we return to in Chapter 8.

Finally, we have looked at the health and well-being needs of the group. Evidence of need, particularly in terms of emotional and behavioural issues (including substance misuse and offending) and mental health problems, highlighted the vulnerability of the group. While most of these young people were receiving generic support to address their difficulties, it appeared that more specialist and focused help was not always in place.

Notes

1 The legislative base for leaving care work differs across the UK. The Children Act 1989 provides a base for services in England and Wales. This was adapted in Scotland in the throughcare and aftercare provisions of the Children (Scotland) Act 1995 and in Northern Ireland through the Children (Northern Ireland) Order 1995. More recently the implementation of the Children (Leaving Care) Act 2000 in England and Wales has brought about a re-shaping of leaving care services. Similar measures have been implemented in Scotland and Northern Ireland.

2 In our study we have used the term independence to mean a move to a council or housing association tenancy, a private flat or bed-sit, to supported lodgings or a hostel, to friends or other temporary arrangements (without 24-hour staff cover). Young people who remained with foster carers on a supported lodgings basis, however, were treated separately and not included in the category of having moved to independent living. Unlike some other forms of independent living, remaining with foster carers after legal discharge (i.e. as supported carers) is seen a means of offering a 'flexible needs led approach to the timing of leaving care' (Wade 1997) which may provide stability and continuity at a crucial stage in the lives of care leavers. In the current study, remaining with foster carers accounted for 6.5 per cent of the young people in the total sample, 9.1 per cent of the Shire sample and 8.5 per cent of the City sample.

3 Recent developments in legislation (implemented in 2004) introduced new financial arrangements for young people leaving care. Under the new policy most care leavers under the age of 18 are no longer eligible to claim income support or housing benefit. Social services have instead taken on the responsibility for financial support (see Chapter 9). The study was conducted before the new financial arrangements came into place.

Chapter 6

Supporting Young People: Aftercare

Introduction

We have already touched upon some aspects of support for young people as they move on from care. In this chapter we focus more closely on the help and aftercare support they received as they continued the transition from care to independent living. We look at formal sources of support, including aftercare support from social workers and leaving care workers. We also consider informal sources of support from family, friends and ex-carers and the importance of building and maintaining social networks. First, however, we present a general overview of the policy context for delivering aftercare support across local authorities in Scotland.

Aftercare

> Aftercare is the provision of advice, guidance and assistance when a young person ceases to be looked after. (The Children (Scotland) Act 1995 Regulations and Guidance, Vol. 2)

Section 29 of the Children (Scotland) Act 1995 places a duty on local authorities to provide aftercare to those young people looked after at school leaving age up until they reach 19 years of age. Authorities also have the power to provide aftercare up to 21 years of age. It has been well documented that the transition to independent living can be a difficult and isolating process for looked after young people. While effective 'throughcare' may prepare the young person for this transition, they will require continued support via a range of accessible and flexible aftercare services. During our national survey of local authorities we explored aftercare provision in five key life areas. These included personal support and special needs, accommodation, finance, career and health.

Personal support

Continuity and consistency of service can offer a safe and familiar environment in which young people can begin the transition to independence. In our survey, in most (94%) of our authorities, young people were able to continue in foster care placements after legally leaving care (two of these authorities, however, noted that this would be in exceptional circumstances only). This approach represents a positive step in helping to promote continuity and stability for young people at this important stage in their lives.

We also found that a third (10) of authorities reported having formal policies in relation to providing a continuing care role for foster and residential carers. Examples included financial recompense appropriate to the level of continued input (e.g. travel expenses and revised fees) and the use of residential units as designated contact points for care leavers. Of the 20 authorities who said they did not have formal policies, 10 per cent said that arrangements could be made on an individual basis to facilitate a continued care role: for example, the use of residential workers to provide continuing outreach work.

A respondent from one authority that did not have a formal policy for facilitating a continuing care role highlighted the problems of an unplanned 'open to return' approach. They commented on the potential disruption caused to other residents by allowing young people to return to residential units and noted that 'Support via the through care team is preferred method of response. Staff and carers are not disinterested but do have a recognisable "new focus".'

An important part of ensuring consistency in support is the allocation of a named person to continue contact with care leavers. Most of the local authorities (87%) provided young people with a named contact. Most (71%) used specialist leaving care workers to maintain contact with care leavers, although field social workers and residential workers were also widely used (in 55% and 35% of authorities respectively). In over a quarter (29%) of these authorities all three were identified as ongoing contacts depending on the most appropriate for the individual young person. Other specialist staff who were involved in continuing contact included Social Inclusion Partnership (SIP) mentors, project workers and a homemaker.

We found that in addition to providing named contact staff, authorities employed a variety of strategies to continue contact with care leavers. Arrangements included referring young people to the throughcare teams or providing formal packages of support. Drop-in centres were mentioned, as were group activities, advice for young people on how to access services and a proactive staff approach. Examples of the latter included planned and unplanned visits, phone calls, letters and invitations to outings and Christmas celebrations. Two authorities mentioned developing more effective tracking systems. One of these suggested employing an incentive for yearly contact, such as a birthday present or meal.

ENDING PERSONAL SUPPORT

Local authorities were also asked to outline their policy on ending personal support services. Around 80 per cent of authorities operated a flexible approach to ending personal support. The majority commented that support generally ended by mutual agreement or at the young person's request. Around half operated an open door policy which allowed young people to self-refer or be re-referred for support and in some cases return to care. Drop-in centres were also mentioned as a means of continuing *informal* support and contact. Only three authorities outlined more formal procedures. These included decisions to end support being taken by social workers and line managers, the arrangement of an exit interview and ending support six months after the young person's move to independence. One authority simply stated 'age'.

Aftercare support for special needs

As explored in the previous chapter, some care leavers will have additional or special needs that extend beyond the level of general provision for young people leaving care. Local authorities were asked to indicate whether they provided specialist support initiatives or specialist accommodation to those young people who had particular needs. Table 6.1 indicates the level of support available across 31 local authorities.

Some authorities who did not have specialist support initiatives for these young people commented that specialist support would be identified and addressed on an individual basis. This was reiterated by a small number of authorities who reported that providing specialist initiatives for these groups was not viable because of the low number of care leavers in their area.

In some cases, specialist accommodation was not specific to care leavers only, but rather specific to the sub-groups mentioned and open to young people who were leaving or had left care. For example, one authority respondent noted that: 'A voluntary agency provides shared supported accommodation for young women with babies which will accept care leavers. The Social Work Department provides staffed supported accommodation for young people with mental health problems who may be care leavers.'

Table 6.1 Authorities offering specialist services for care leavers

Care leaver sub-groups	Authorities providing specialist support	Authorities providing or arranging specialist accommodation
Young people from ethnic backgrounds	0	1
Young parents	7	13
Physically disabled young people	3	8
Learning disabled young people	5	12
Young people with mental health problems	7	11
Young people with substance misuse problems	5	5
Young offenders	8	7

Accommodation

The considerable work undertaken by local authorities to address the accommodation needs of care leavers reflects the high priority afforded to the area of aftercare. Nearly three-quarters of authorities (74%) reported having formal agreements with the housing department or housing providers in respect of accommodating care leavers.[1]

Strategies included:

- provision of supported flats for care leavers and, in some cases, other vulnerable young people

- multi-agency involvement in committees, and the review and evaluation of care packages aimed at young people's housing needs

- involvement of housing departments in care reviews to assess 'special needs points' early to ensure continuity of service (e.g. joint assessment protocols)

- joint homelessness strategy to target care leavers and other vulnerable young people.

Two of the authorities that did not have formal agreements did have informal working arrangements with the housing department or housing providers in respect of accommodating care leavers. Also, one authority was in the process of negotiating a formal agreement involving the voluntary sector and Housing Department.

Young people leaving care will have diverse accommodation needs according to their individual circumstances and their ability to cope independently. Overall, we found that authorities were able to offer a good range of accommodation *options* to young people. Availability was not explored in this survey. Most (84%) authorities provided four or more options. Thirteen per cent currently had three accommodation options for care leavers, and 3 per cent offered only two options.

As Table 6.2 indicates, the most common types of accommodation for care leavers in Scotland were independent tenancies (94%), supported lodgings (90%) and remaining with foster carers on a supported lodgings basis (90%).[2] Foyers were not so widely used, with only 10 per cent of authorities offering this type of accommodation.

Table 6.2 Accommodation options for care leavers

Accommodation type	Number of authorities offering accommodation type (n=31)
Foster carers providing supported lodgings	28
Supported lodgings	28
Supported hostel	20
Accommodation with floating support	22
Semi-independent flats (with 24-hour support)	21
Independent tenancies	29
Foyers	3
Other	10

'Other' accommodation options included semi-independent flats with eight-hour support, student flats for care leavers who attend college, a mother and baby unit, bed and breakfasts and a range of supported accommodation tied to particular initiatives.

Ideally, a young person's personal preference should be considered alongside their assessed needs and level of ability. Almost all authorities indicated their commitment to observing the wishes of young people in the provision of accommodation. Although somewhat limited in detail, responses suggested that views were generally sought via the care plans and the review process. One authority respondent stated, 'Unfortunately, we are seldom in a position to offer choice. Where we can the young person is the decision maker.' Another outlined their approach to ensuring that young people were able to make an informed choice. 'Young people are involved from the start in the selection. They are taken to visit a range of accommodation options and get information from staff and young people who have already moved on.'

A number of authorities indicated their objective to reach a compromise based on the young person's preference, needs and abilities weighed against the availability of suitable accommodation in the local area.

ACCOMMODATION CONTINGENCY PLANS

Most authorities reported that accommodation breakdowns would be dealt with under homeless person legislation and that care leavers would be treated as priority homeless. However, in some cases contingency arrangements seemed somewhat ad hoc, possibly due to availability.

Arrangements included the option for return to residential or foster care or re-admittance to an independent flat or residential options, depending on availability. A number of authorities provided emergency accommodation via the housing department or voluntary schemes, or had access to hotels as a temporary measure. Bed and breakfasts tended to be used as a last resort.

Three authorities highlighted an out of hours resource, where young people were offered advice and support from either a duty social worker or throughcare worker. In one authority an emergency throughcare response involved arranging temporary accommodation and financial assistance and exploring long-term options with the young person. Another operated a crisis team and emergency hostel accommodation.

Finance

As we have seen, poor educational attainment and low participation in training and employment amongst care leavers suggests that this group of young people is likely to be financially dependent on benefits for some time after leaving care (Biehal *et al.* 1995; Broad 1998). In order that young people moving from care to independence do so with the full financial resources available to them, certain measures should be in place. For example, local authorities have specific powers under Sections 29 and 30 of the Children (Scotland) Act to provide financial assistance to care leavers. However, the discretionary features of these powers necessitate the development of a clear authority policy in respect of financial assistance. This should outline the eligibility criteria, assessment and application procedures and the range and extent of provision available under Sections 29 and 30 payments as well as from mainstream sources.

Of the 31 authorities, 26 per cent supplied detailed accounts of policy in this area, addressing these issues. Almost a quarter (23%) simply stated that policy was in accordance with Section 29. Several authorities reported that financial assistance was based on individual need but gave little or no indication of how this would be assessed.

Such limited information made it difficult to ascertain the extent to which policy varied across authorities. It seemed, however, that a common theme was to explore all existing mainstream sources before allocating Section 29 or 30 funds. A number of authorities commented that they would conduct a 'maximising income' check to ensure that young people were accessing their full entitlements and would provide top-up payments to subsidise or fill in gaps between mainstream sources.

RANGE OF PROVISION

In terms of the range of financial support, just over two-thirds (67%) of authorities said that they offered four or more types of financial assistance to young people leaving care. Only one authority reported that they did not offer any of the types specified in the questionnaire (see Table 6.3). Financial provision for the small number of care leavers in this authority took the form of 'material provision chosen by the young person'.

As indicated in Table 6.3, the most widely available form of financial assistance was leaving care grants, with most of the authorities (90%) reporting that they provided this type of assistance. A small number of these (13%) made a standard payment to young people leaving care. In one case this consisted of a £2500 start-up payment for moving into their own home and, in another, a grant of £1000 was given to young people who had been looked after by the authority. In the latter case, some of the amount was to be repaid if the young person went on to receive a community care grant.

'Other' forms of assistance included crisis or destitution payments, food parcels, clothing, items required for young people in custody, money for driving lessons and leisure activities and, in one authority, holidays.

Table 6.3 Types of financial assistance
available in local authorities

Financial assistance type	Number of authorities offering financial assistance (n=30)
Leaving care grant	28
Income top-up	20
Education assistance	24
Employment assistance	11
Accommodation subsidies	27
Other	8

Overall, this provides a clear indication that social work departments are playing an important role in providing financial assistance to care leavers in several areas of their lives. Their total expenditure on financial assistance ranged from £6000 in one of the smaller authorities to £1,935,030. However, many authorities were unable to provide a breakdown of spending on each of the specified types of financial assistance.

INFORMATION

Young people should be equipped with information about their financial and income entitlements. We found that the level and sources of information varied across local authorities from providing clear and easy to understand leaflets on accessing and managing an income, to relying on verbal information from staff.

Two authorities supplied comprehensive information as part of a leaving care pack, which outlined entitlements, explained the range of benefits available to care leavers and provided useful numbers and addresses for accessing further information.

Just over a tenth (16%) of authorities reported that they carried out income and benefit maximisation checks with individual young people leaving care, to ensure that they were receiving their full entitlements. Other methods of providing information included: access to the welfare rights team and money advisors; advising young people during the course of preparation work on what was available to them through the social work department and other sources; and the dissemination of printed material from relevant agencies. Several authorities commented that they were in the process of addressing this issue or developing information.

WORKING LINKS

In our study we found that over half (52%) of authorities had no formal working arrangements in respect of income entitlements. Of the 14 authorities who reported having such arrangements, 8 had links with the Benefits Agency, 13 had links with housing and 3 had links with education. Under half (39%) of the authorities who responded to our questionnaire had a designated member of staff responsible for financial assistance.

Careers, education, employment and training

One of the 'milestones' outlined in the Scottish Executive's *Social Justice* document is 'halving the proportion of 16 to 19 year olds who are not in education, training or employment' (Scottish Executive 2000c). This has particular implications for looked after young people and care leavers who, research indicates, are particularly disadvantaged in terms of educational attainment and participation in training and employment.

Just under two-thirds (19) of local authorities said that they had a strategy for helping care leavers into education, employment and training. Arrangements included accessing advice and assistance from careers or education services as part of throughcare or preparation work, offering financial assistance for further or higher education and specific agreements with the careers service, such as ring-fencing skill seekers' placements or providing specialist employment-related support for 15- to 24-year-olds who have been in care.

STRATEGY

Just over a quarter of authorities (26%) offered specialist projects providing basic skills and employment-related support for looked after young people and care leavers. Provision varied from voluntary schemes, such as the Prince's Trust, to SIP initiatives and in-house projects run by the throughcare team or social work department. Although not all of these projects were exclusive to care leavers, the majority adopted a holistic approach to developing skills and while the main focus was on employability, wider issues – such as accommodation, substance misuse, health and emotional well-being and personal development – were also addressed.

FORMAL ARRANGEMENTS

In relation to assisting young people to acquire new skills and increase access to education, employment and training, just over half (55%) of authorities said they had formal arrangements with education, careers, employment or training providers. Five of these consisted of input from relevant agencies in the preparation process or as part of SIP initiatives. Twelve involved linking up with these agencies to provide training programmes or to arrange placements. Examples included college taster courses and vocational or pre-vocational training run by various council schemes or voluntary agencies, such as the Prince's Trust, National Children's Homes (NCH) and Apex Trust.

The majority of authorities (61%) reported providing young people with information on education, training and employment although this varied across authorities. In some, information was provided in specific sections of leaving care packs. For example, two authorities reported using the National Foster Care Association (NFCA) *Stepping Out* material while a further three authorities had developed their own leaving care resource packs.

Information was also supplied through direct contact with either staff from careers companies or the various training schemes. Pamphlets, newsletters and college prospectuses from careers, education and other relevant agencies were also widely used. Only one authority mentioned making computer facilities available as a means of accessing information. Almost a quarter of authorities (23%) relied mostly on verbal information from social work or throughcare staff as part of the care planning and preparation process. Only two authorities said they had no specific information at present and one authority commented that it was an ongoing task to develop this area.

Health

Finally, we also looked at aftercare provision in the key area of health. As we have seen in previous chapters, evidence indicates that care leavers have significant health care needs. It is reported that, as a group, they have high levels of smoking, alcohol and drug use and high levels of chronic physical conditions and mental health problems. The high incidence of early parenthood also indicates a need for advice on sexual health (Stein and Wade 2000).

The Children (Scotland) Act 1995 Regulations and Guidance Volume 2 suggests that:

When a young person ceases to be looked after, an assessment should be made of their health needs and clarification of whether any special services need to be in place for them. (Chapter 7, para. 58)

It also suggests that young people should be encouraged to follow a healthy lifestyle and to access the services offered by the primary health care team.

In our policy survey 42 per cent of local authorities reported having formal agreements with health organisations to promote the health and development of young people who had been looked after. Arrangements were mainly with the local health promotions unit.

We also found that just under half (48%) of authorities reported having a strategy for promoting a healthy and stable lifestyle for looked after young people and care leavers. Approaches to health included one-to-one support, group work on specific health issues, the provision of funds to facilitate sport and recreational activities, and information on healthy eating and exercise contained within throughcare and leaving care resource packs. Almost a fifth of authorities (19%) appeared to rely solely on the care planning process or the LAC material to address this issue. Only three authorities outlined specific health programmes. These consisted of: a specific project to work on health development and to promote and increase access to health services targeted at young people looked after and previously looked after; a healthy living project which was a joint initiative run over 13 weeks in a homeless unit; and input from a health visitor during support work sessions with care leavers.

Interpretations of what a health strategy should involve varied considerably across authorities. For example, some authorities that said they did not have a health strategy did in fact have some input from health staff either directly (e.g. group talks) or through SIP initiatives. Several authorities indicated that the development of strategies with health promotion and other services such as psychiatry were being pursued.

In terms of specific health and personal development needs, just under half (48%) of the authorities reported that they had initiatives for working with care leavers on specific issues. Around a third (35%) had programmes for dealing with sexual health and/or sexuality, 32 per cent had projects for drug and alcohol related issues and 26 per cent addressed leisure activities.

Of the 16 authorities that did not report specific initiatives, several pointed out that health and personal development issues were nevertheless dealt with as part of the preparation process prior to leaving care.

Aftercare support in practice
Having looked at the policy context for providing aftercare support, we now turn to young people's experience of support from both formal and informal sources in our three authorities.

Formal support: aftercare support at baseline
Providing effective support in the months after moving on relies on continued contact with support workers (whether social workers or leaving care workers). Information gathered for the sample as a whole (n= 107) revealed that around three in five young people had such contact at the point of entry to the study, although the level and intensity of support varied. For example, around a fifth (22%) of young people said they had contact with both a social worker and a leaving care worker. Just under a fifth (19%), meanwhile, had contact with a leaving care worker only and 12 per cent had contact with a social worker only. Around two in five (38%) young people, however, reported that they had no contact with either a social worker or a leaving care worker, a disconcerting finding given the importance placed on aftercare support.

As outlined earlier, young people in the full sample had left care between 1 and 24 months prior to joining the study (although the average was six months). They were therefore at different stages of their transition from care at the time of supplying this information. It may be expected that support may lessen over time as young people become more independent. However, analysis indicated that the number of months since moving on from care had no significant effect on whether or not a young person had contact with a social worker or leaving care worker. This implies that some young people who had recently left care were just as likely to have no contact with a support worker as those who had left care over a year ago.

Contact with support workers over the follow-up period
Additional information on aftercare support from social workers and leaving care workers was collected from the group of young people who took part in the six-month follow-up study (n=61). Contact and support were explored at both baseline (at the point of joining the study, referred to as T1) and again at the six-month outcome point (referred to as T2). The pattern of responses is shown in Table 6.4.

At baseline, an average for the follow-up group of five months after moving on from care, just over two-fifths (41%) reported contact with either a social worker or a leaving care worker. A similar proportion (39%) of young people had no contact with either. We also found evidence that some young people were unsure as to who was working with them. For example, 6 per cent said they had a leaving care worker but weren't sure whether they still had a social worker and 5 per cent were not sure whether they had been allocated a leaving care worker. Some were not sure who was supporting them. This suggests the need for clearer procedures when allocating support and when ending contact with a young person and also for greater clarity when explaining the roles and responsibilities of those involved in providing support.

Table 6.4 Contact with support workers at baseline and at follow-up

	Baseline (T1) %	Follow-up (T2) %
Leaving care worker only	13	25
Social worker only	17	8
Both	18	20
Neither	39	44
Not sure*	11	4

*Some young people had a social worker but weren't sure if they had a specialist leaving care worker and vice versa.

Information gathered for the follow-up group at T2 (an average of 11 months after moving on from care) showed that in total 30 per cent still had contact with a social worker and around half (47%) still had contact with a leaving care worker. However, as Table 6.4 indicates, over two in five young people (44%) did not have contact with either.

Further analysis of contact with support workers showed some degree of change in contact within individual cases. For example, 17 per cent of the follow-up group had lost contact with either their social worker, leaving care worker or both over the six-month follow-up. A quarter, meanwhile, had maintained contact with their support worker(s) throughout the follow-up and 13 per cent reported improved contact by T2. Changes in the patterns of contact may reflect a tendency for contact to increase at times of difficulty and to fall away over time. It may also reflect the tendency to decrease support for those who are perceived to be more settled. For example, as we discuss in the next chapter, there was some evidence that young people who remained or returned home to parents had less intervention from these key support workers.

Exploring whether young people had contact with support workers provides some indication of whether such support was present or lacking in their lives. In order to explore the intensity of this support, young people who still had contact with a social worker or leaving care worker at T2 were asked how often they met with them. As shown in Table 6.5, responses indicated that young people tended to have more frequent contact with their leaving care worker. It is likely that this reflects the tendency for social workers to withdraw intensive work with young people as leaving care workers become more involved. There was also some indication that where social workers continued to provide considerable support it was in the absence of input from other professionals. For example, half of those who met with their social worker on a weekly basis did not have contact with a leaving care worker.

Table 6.5 Percentage of young people who had contact with support workers at T2 and frequency of contact

	Social worker	Leaving care worker
Weekly	25	57
Fortnightly	5	16
Monthly	25	20
Less often	45	7

The nature of this contact was also explored to see whether there were any differences in the way contact was organised and arranged between social workers and leaving care workers. Just under half of those with a social worker said that most contact tended to be organised at the young person's request (44% of cases). For the remaining cases, most contact was either planned by the worker (28%) or in an emergency (28%). For those who had contact with a leaving care worker, the majority (74%) said that contact was planned and regular and organised by the support worker. This reflects the responsibility of leaving care services to maintain contact with care leavers and provide aftercare support.

Young people's experiences of aftercare support

The helpfulness of support from social workers and leaving care workers was explored by a number of different means. This involved asking young people to identify the areas in which information and support had been provided and asking them to comment directly on how helpful or useful their contact with support workers had been.

INFORMATION AND SUPPORT WITH LIFE AREAS

Young people in the study were asked whether they had received support or information from their support workers in key life skill areas since leaving care. Figure 6.1 illustrates responses from the total sample (n=107). It shows that leaving care workers, as one would expect, were particularly instrumental in supporting young people across the main life areas after care. However, it also shows that social workers continued to play a signifi-cant part in supporting some young people.

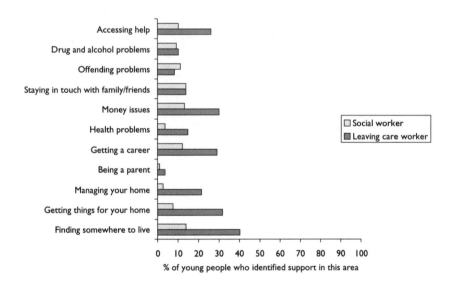

Figure 6.1 Support with key life areas from social workers and specialist leaving care workers

Many young people appeared not to have received help from support workers across key life areas (around 60% or more). As we have seen, however, some young people did not have contact with support workers and others may not have required support in certain areas of their life; for example, those without children would not necessarily require support with parenting. However, it was apparent that there were certain areas of focus for support workers. A significant area for support, certainly from leaving care workers, was housing issues, whether it involved help to find accommodation, assistance in managing and sustaining accommodation or overseeing and assisting in the purchase of furnishings. Other major areas included help with money, finding a career and accessing other sources of support. There was also evidence that support could be holistic, as some young people who had difficulties with health, offending or substance misuse had received support from their social worker or leaving care worker with these issues.

It was also apparent that some young people would have welcomed more information and support from their social worker or leaving care worker in certain key areas. Table 6.6 shows the percentage of young people who said they would have liked more help. Priority areas included help with managing their money, finding a career and help with housing.

Table 6.6 Areas in which more support was requested

	% of young people
Money and budgeting	47
Finding a career	39
Finding somewhere to live	34
Developing skills for adult life	33
Managing your home	29
Keeping in touch with family and friends	19
Health issues	10
Parenting or childcare issues	7

Young men were more likely than young women to have wanted further support with keeping in touch with family and friends (24% compared to 17% of young women), managing a home (42% compared to 27%) and finding either education, training or work (50% compared to 35%). We also found that a greater number of young people in County authority would have liked more help from their social worker or specialist leaving care worker with finding somewhere to live (53% compared to 37% in City and 21% in Shire).

Table 6.7 Helpfulness of contact with support workers

	Leaving care worker	Social worker
Very helpful	62	47
Some help	35	40
Never helpful	3	13

HOW HELPFUL WAS CONTACT AND SUPPORT?

Those young people in the follow-up study who were still in contact with a social worker or leaving care worker at T2 were asked whether this contact had been helpful over the follow-up period. As Table 6.7 shows, most young people felt that it had been, although overall support from leaving care workers was perceived more positively.

Young people were also asked to describe their experience of support. Most simply listed the main aspects of help e.g. 'help with money' or 'help with getting my own house'. However, some young people were able to sum up their wider experience of contact with social work and leaving care staff.

There were a number of positive comments about help from support workers. Emma, for example, was still in contact with her leaving care worker a year on from leaving care. Emma felt that she could have used more support in the early stages: 'I had to find out everything on my own as throughcare [services] hadn't met me by the time I had moved out of care.' However, contact had improved over the follow-up period and at T2 she reported meeting with her leaving care worker once every month just to check that things were OK. Emma felt that this was sufficient 'because I'm quite capable of running a house now and don't always need support or advice'. She was also in touch with her social worker even though formal involvement had ceased 18 months earlier. 'I see my social worker more socially now...we always got on very well.' In terms of her overall experience of the support she had received, Emma told us: 'The stereotypes of care is not really what it's all about at all. Social workers are not bad devils, they are looking after your best interests.'

Sharon had also received support from her social worker and leaving care worker over the follow-up period. She felt that her leaving care worker had been particularly helpful. 'She helps me with cooking, cleaning and showing me how bills work out. Although she sometimes goes over stuff I already know and know how to do, it's helping me work towards getting my own flat.' In terms of support from her social worker, Sharon had mixed feelings; she told us:

> In the time I've been in care I feel that lots of people try to help in every way they can. Although some social workers didn't seem to help as much as others, you always got that social workers would try hard for your sake.

Carrie, who had been looked after at home on a supervision requirement, had formally ceased contact with her social worker at T1. She told us, 'My social worker was a great help to my family and I.' Since her supervision requirement ended, Carrie had moved to her own tenancy and had received weekly support from a leaving care worker which she found very helpful. 'She reminds me to do things, listens to my problems and answers my questions and she helped me with my new house.'

Some young people had less positive experiences of support. Several described a decrease in contact, while others had found their support workers unhelpful. Common themes included feeling let down and unsupported.

Brett had been looked after at home and at T2, eight months after leaving care, he had no support workers. He told us: 'I felt abandoned when the supervision order was removed. I never knew my social worker. I never saw him even though I was on a supervision order.' Brett had not been allocated a leaving care worker and in summing up his experience of being in care he said: 'Don't look for help from the social services, it's not there.'

Charlie was also dissatisfied with the support he had received during the time he had been looked after by his aunt. At T2, just under a year after leaving care, he had not had contact with his social worker for several months. He told us:

> I never got much help from the social work; whenever my aunt asked for anything for me she was told it would take time, then it was forgotten about. My social worker was never any use to me; they thought because I was with my family I would be alright. If and when they visited me the visit would last five minutes. At the last social work meeting, the day I came off my order, we were promised a visit from them to help me and we were never contacted again. The social work department never helped me in any way.

Iris's comments about her experience highlight the importance of consistency and empathy when providing support. When asked why she no longer had contact with any support workers at T2 she told us:

There was one social worker who was quite good but he had to leave. I didn't get on with the other ones; it was all different workers all the time. I think what is needed is for more social workers to have had experiences of not going to school and being in care – it might mean they'd have more understanding of how it feels for young people.

Other criticisms included difficulties in contacting support workers. Some support workers had failed to turn up for pre-arranged visits either on time or at all and others were unavailable when young people had tried to contact them. While this clearly raises issues relating to resources and workloads, it nevertheless illustrates some of the problems young people had in accessing support.

Gill had seen her social worker a few times since leaving residential school over a year ago; however, she was unsure whether contact had now formally ended: 'My previous social worker has left and I've not been allocated another one, I don't really know if I will be.' Over the follow-up period Gill had been referred to the leaving care team but had only met her leaving care worker on two occasions in six months. At T2 Gill was feeling isolated and unsupported. Although she acknowledged that she needed support, she felt unmotivated to push for it.

My support worker is very difficult to get hold of. She is either ill or in a meeting. I haven't spoke to or seen her in a few months now. She hasn't contacted me and I haven't contacted her. It's not helpful when she's not available at the agreed time because something else has come up. There should be more people out there for young people to talk to, more people to help them out. When you are in care, you've got the staff to help you; when you're out, you've just got yourself.

The underlying aim of aftercare is to make sure that no young person feels unsupported and alone. While there will be occasions when support services will have difficulty in engaging young people in aftercare support, it is important that young people are able to access support if and when they require it or are ready to engage.

Finally, young people were asked whether they felt that their support worker had listened to their views. Involving young people in decisions about their lives is a key component of good practice in delivering throughcare and aftercare services and, as we have seen in earlier chapters, overall there was a high level of commitment by local authorities to developing strategies to facilitate consultation with young people. On an individual level, there was also evidence that young people were participating in planning and decisions about their future. Around eight in ten (82%) young people from the follow-up study felt that their support worker had listened to their views.

Effective support from social workers and leaving care workers can make a substantial difference to the lives of young people leaving care. In this next section we explore the equally important role of family and social networks in helping young people to manage their move from care to post-care living.

Informal support

FAMILY

Previous research has highlighted the importance of family contact for positive post-care outcomes, whether it be successful reintegration into the family unit or the provision of an emotional, practical and financial support network for those living independently (Marsh and Peel 1999; Morgan-Klein 1985; Stein and Carey 1986). The Children (Scotland) Act 1995 seeks to reinforce the idea of joint parenting by promoting the continued role of parents and family for children who are looked after, through the rights and responsibilities of parents towards their children and by emphasising the role of social work services in encouraging and maintaining family links, where appropriate.

Information gathered for all young people (n=107) at the point of entry to the study showed that 90 per cent reported having some form of contact with their birth family. However, 43 per cent of these young people were living with one or both parents at the time of reporting. Of those young people who lived away from their family, most (84%) reported having contact with them. Contact included visits, telephone calls and information exchanged via other family members or friends.

Young people were also asked to indicate which family members they saw on a regular basis (i.e. at least every two weeks). As Table 6.8 illustrates, most young people (57%) saw their birth mother at least every two weeks, however, over half (52%) of these young people were living at home. Analysis carried out on those young people who were living away from home showed that just under half (45%) saw their mother this often. Meeting with siblings, however, was more evident for young people whether living at home or away from home. Overall, almost two-thirds (63%) reported seeing a brother or sister on a regular basis.

For some young people, maintaining contact with family had proved difficult since being in care. A number expressed the desire to see family members more often or to establish contact with those they had lost touch with.

Table 6.8 Regular meetings with family members

	% of young people
Siblings	63
Birth mother	57
Birth father	39
Grandparents	36
Aunts/uncles	31
Other family member	12
Stepdad	8
Stepmum	7
Adoptive family	1

Denise lived some distance from her mother and although she kept in touch by phone she had not seen her mum in several months. Occasionally she had received financial help from the leaving care worker to visit her mum and told us: 'I wish she was closer, she's really understanding, really supportive, she's happy with whatever decisions I make with my life.'

Corrine had no contact with her family at T1. She told us that one of the bad things about her life was not being able to see her siblings, 'I don't get to see any of my siblings 'coz of my mum's fault and I think I'm getting punished for something she done. I hope one day I'll get to see my brothers and sister.' Barry had also lost touch with some family members. Although he had regular contact with his dad at T1, he had lost touch at T2. He was also trying to re-establish contact with his mum and grandparents. He told us, 'My social worker has tried to get my gran and mum to talk to me but there's the family dispute. I hope to eventually be on talking terms with my family, have family and friends around me.'

In terms of contact with extended family, around a third saw grandparents and aunts and uncles at least every fortnight (36% and 31% respectively). Over a tenth (12 %) saw 'other' family members, such as cousins and stepsiblings.

Young people were also asked to specify which family member they felt closest to. Just under half (45%) identified their mother, with siblings (17%) being the second most common response. Over a tenth (16%) of those young people who felt closest to their mother, however, did not see her on a regular basis.

In terms of emotional and practical support, 44 per cent of young people said that they could turn to a family member if something went wrong in their life. Parents were cited most commonly, but siblings, grandparents and aunts featured prominently. Around half (51%) of those who said they had someone they could talk to if they were feeling unhappy or lonely, felt that they could talk to a relative.

Overall, many young people in our study reported links with immediate and extended family and most (97%) found contact helpful. There was some difference in opinion from support workers, some of whom did not always agree that a young person's contact with their family was helpful (only 66% of family contact was rated as helpful by support workers). Nevertheless, the extent of family contact reported by young people demonstrates the considerable effort of social workers and leaving care workers to promote, encourage and facilitate ongoing contact with family.

FRIENDS AND SOCIAL NETWORKS

Friends and social contacts can also be an important source of emotional and practical support. The feeling that one is part of a group can be both reassuring and important for self-esteem and identity. Although the quality and nature of friendships were not explored in detail, we were able to draw upon the perceptions of young people to provide an overview of the pattern of social networks and informal social support.

Most (82%) of the young people reported having one or more close friendships at the point of entering the study. This was more so for young women than young men (55% and 49% respectively). Around two in ten, however, had either some friends but no one close (13%) or no real friends at all (5%). Brian, for example, had some friends, but he added, 'I know them from hostels, homes, my old home area. I couldn't rely on them, though.' Several young people mentioned the problem of losing friends through a change in their circumstances. Helen said she had no close friends at T2. 'I had quite a lot of friends...some I'd see more often than others but because I'm pregnant I can't go out the same and socialise with them.' Lucy, meanwhile, had moved to a different town when she left care. At T2 she also said that she had no real friends:

> I miss the group of friends I had. I had quite a lot of friends, but I moved area and I'm one for working a lot so I had a job that involved getting up early and working late. So basically my friends lost interest, because I wasn't going out. They kind of just dumped me, you know.

Just over a tenth (15%) of young people said they could turn to a friend for help if something went wrong in their life and almost half (47%) said that if they were feeling sad, depressed or lonely, they had a friend they could talk to. Carrie, for example, referred to her friends often when talking about support. She said, 'I've known my main friends for over five years, before care, and can rely on them for advice, guidance and support.' Many young people had experience of long-term friendships both with friends they had met before care as well as through being in care. Craig had a number of close friends:

> One of my good friends I have known since I was born. I have only one friend that I have known through care. The rest of my pals I have known since leaving care. Most of my friends give me help when I need it. They listen to me when I have problems.

Just over a fifth (21%) of young people who had been looked after away from home said that they had stayed in touch with young people they had lived with, as in Nicola's case. 'My best friend, six years I've known her. Met her when I was in foster care and could ask her for advice, talk to her about almost anything.'

Although for most young people friends represented a positive influence in their lives, some highlighted the negative side of friendships, such as peer pressure, hanging around with the wrong crowd or getting involved in trouble. One young person found that trying to make a new start for himself by staying out of trouble had brought isolation from friends, most of whom were involved in offending:

> Most of my friends are in jail, I'd say three close friends and they're all locked up and I don't have any real friends now 'coz I've moved on a bit. If I kept on going the way I was going, I was going to end up with them.

Where support was available from family and social networks, it was clearly valued by young people. When asked to talk about the good aspects of their life, many mentioned their partners, friends and family. Jay said the positive aspects of his life at T2 were 'my girlfriend and my baby boy'. Tracey also appreciated her family and friends:

> The good things in my life at the moment is I am getting on much better with my family; my sister has got a baby who I am going to see and I have a

new home of my own and I am engaged to my boyfriend. Everything is happy.

Phil was living at home and was not receiving any professional support at T2. However, despite difficulties with finding work and sorting out his finances, he felt very positive about his life and told us the good things 'are my family, they are good to me. My mum keeps me going with money and things; she does a lot for me and I like my friends and I managed to get a ticket for the Rangers game.'

Sharon also felt well supported by friends, family and her support carer:

Just now I have plenty of friends who I can trust and a boyfriend who I like very much. I am happy where I stay and the amount of contact I have with my sister and brother. I get on well with my carer. She helps me a lot.

Support from ex-carers

Support from ex-carers crosses the boundary between formal and informal support. Carers and ex-carers may form an important part of the network of social support for young people leaving care. However, under a third (29%) of young people who had been looked after away from home were still in touch with ex-residential workers or foster carers at the point of joining the study, an average of six months after leaving care.

Furthermore, there was some indication that contact had decreased over time. Information from those young people in the follow-up study who had been looked after away from home showed that two-fifths (40%) still had regular contact with an ex-foster or residential carer at T1; however, under a third (27%) reported contact at T2. The decrease in contact was particularly apparent in relation to reports of contact with residential workers, which fell from 24 per cent of young people at T1 to 10 per cent at T2.

Those young people who did have continued contact identified positive examples of ongoing support, such as calling round for a chat or for dinner and telephone calls just to catch up. Robin had monthly telephone contact with his ex-foster carers: 'I enjoy just talking to them on the phone; they are still taking an interest in what I'm doing now and offer advice.'

Lucy had lived with her foster carers for five years prior to leaving care. When things didn't work out in her first flat she was able to move back to her foster parents until new accommodation was found. At T2, ten months on from moving to independent living, Lucy still saw her foster carers every three weeks or so. In describing her ongoing relationship with them, she said:

> I have close contact, mainly over the phone but try to keep in contact and see them. I know I can talk to my foster parents 'coz I have a close relationship to them and I have a relationship with their son 'coz I was there since the day he was born. At the end of it, my foster family, they basically were there for me no matter what happened, they are always there.

Donald still had contact with his ex-residential workers six months on from leaving care. Although he did not see them on a regular basis, it was nevertheless important for him to know that he could call in and see them:

> Once in a while I visit the unit, sometimes I go there to see certain members of staff, some were good to me. I get on well with quite a few so it's a two-way thing, me going down, I want to go and they are happy for me to go.

Ongoing contact can represent continuity and consistency of support for young people moving on from care. However, maintaining contact may be affected by young people's personal choice, as in Sheila's case: 'I don't have contact with the residential staff – there's no point – they were doing their job, now they've done their job.' It may also be influenced by their post-care circumstances: 'My relationship with the foster family broke down, I don't talk to them now.' A further barrier to continued contact is the subsequent responsibilities of foster carers and residential workers as they take on the care of other looked after young people. One leaving care manager, commenting on the difficulties of organising ongoing support from ex-carers, noted, 'staff and carers are not disinterested but do have a recognisable new focus'.

Conclusion

Our policy survey showed that local authorities were providing or accessing a range of aftercare services for young people. This included personal support, accommodation, finance, education and careers and health care.

Key personal support issues are providing opportunities for young people to remain in foster care during their transition to adulthood, promoting continuity of care through contact with former carers and the need for more formal procedures for ending personal support.

Our survey revealed the high priority afforded to meet the accommodation needs of care leavers. In addition to several joint housing and social work departments, most authorities had formal agreements with housing providers and access to a range of accommodation plus support options, from supported lodgings to independent tenancies. Also, in most authorities care leavers were treated as a priority group under the homeless persons legislation.

As regards financial support, although most authorities were providing different forms of support, there was often a lack of transparency in respect of their arrangements. Also, more could be done in providing information to young people, ensuring they receive their full income entitlements and developing formal relationships with the Benefits Agency.

Arrangements for helping young people into education, employment and training were very variable – as many as 40 per cent of our authorities responded that they did not have a strategy, and the same percentage did not provide young people with information on education, employment or training.

Most of the local authorities we surveyed recognised that meeting the health needs of young people leaving care required more priority than they had given to it in the past. This should include the introduction of strategies for health promotion and the setting up of formal arrangements with health providers.

With regards to young people's experiences of aftercare, we found that although aftercare provision was available for most young people, those remaining or returning home were often less likely to receive support. Those young people who had received aftercare support generally found it helpful, although budgeting, health and leisure appeared to be given less attention than more traditional areas and a third of young people would have liked more information or help in developing skills for adult life.

Where contact had been maintained, help from leaving care workers was generally viewed more positively than area social workers, although there was some evidence that young people were confused as to who was or should be working with them. Young people's comments about their workers highlighted issues of reliability (turning up late or not at all), following through on commitments, involving young people in decisions and listening to and addressing their needs.

Support from social workers and, to some extent, specialist leaving care workers tended to fall away in the early months after leaving care; again this was particularly so for young people returning to or remaining in the family home. While there was evidence of continuous support throughout the six-month follow-up period for some young people, others had taken up or returned to services at various points after leaving care. Having the option to access and return to these services when in need was, therefore, clearly important.

The importance of family and social networks as sources of support is evident. Certainly, as we shall see in Chapter 8, those young people who lacked a social support network tended to be lacking in self-esteem and well-being and were more likely to cope less well in key life skill areas.

As we have discussed in this chapter, many young people had good links with immediate and extended family and many said that they could turn to family or friends if they needed help or advice. There was also evidence of ongoing contact and support from previous foster and residential carers, although there was a danger of this falling away over time.

Notes

1 Eight authorities reported having joint housing and social work departments.

2 Remaining with foster carers after legal discharge is often referred to as support care or supported lodgings.

Chapter 7

Working Together: Inter-agency Planning and Professional Support

Introduction

As we have seen, at the time of leaving, and after they have left care, many young people need help in finding and sustaining accommodation, accessing health services, securing employment, education or training, and obtaining financial assistance, as well as maintaining any links that are important to them. Their needs will often extend beyond departmental and other agency boundaries.

Section 21 of the Children (Scotland) Act 1995 gives local authority social work departments the power to request the involvement of 'other relevant agencies' from the statutory, voluntary and private sector, in the provision of throughcare and aftercare services. This represents an important step in recognising the pivotal role of multi-agency collaboration, in ensuring that young people receive an effective and efficient service. It is important, therefore, that joint working procedures and assessments are in place to provide as seamless a service as possible.

So far we have looked at support from informal sources (such as family and social networks) and formal sources (such as social workers and leaving care workers). This chapter considers the broader range of professional support agencies that were involved in supporting young people as they moved on from care. It begins by presenting findings from our policy survey on how the different agencies helping young people saw their involvement. It then explores young people's experiences of the support they received.

Leaving care and inter-agency working
Corporate and inter-agency links
CORPORATE PARTNERS

While social work departments have been allocated the lead responsibility for throughcare and aftercare provision, the task of supporting young people who are looked after or leaving care remains a corporate responsibility and as such it is envisaged that housing and education departments will have a role to play. In our policy survey, of the 31 authorities that responded to the questionnaire, 84 per cent reported that the housing department was involved in delivering or overseeing throughcare and aftercare services, although this included eight that were joint housing and social work departments.

EXTERNAL PARTNERS

In terms of formal agreements with external agencies, a similar pattern emerged. As shown in Table 7.1, local authorities were more likely to have links with housing providers than other service providers.

Table 7.1 Formal agreements between social work and other agencies regarding throughcare and aftercare

Formal agreement	Housing providers	Careers	Education and training	Health	Benefits Agency	Children's hearings
Yes	18 (58%)	9 (29%)	7 (23%)	7 (23%)	5 (16%)	4 (13%)
No	13 (42%)	17 (55%)	16 (52%)	19 (61%)	20 (65%)	20 (65%)
Missing response	0	5 (16%)	8 (26%)	5 (16%)	6 (19%)	7 (23%)

In addition to this, 29 per cent of authorities reported having agreements with Social Inclusion Partnerships (SIPs) and 32 per cent had agreements with a range of voluntary organisations, such as Who Cares? Scotland and NCH. One authority reported having a formal agreement with the local criminal justice department. Overall, two-thirds (68 per cent) of the responding authorities reported having formal agreements with one or more of the external agencies. One authority had agreements with all of the specified agencies, including an SIP, while a third indicated that they did not have formal agreements with any of the agencies. This suggests that although a commitment to collaboration with other relevant service providers was a prominent theme in the Children's Services Plans, it has yet to be formalised in almost a third of the authorities we surveyed.

Inter-agency planning

In our survey, over three-quarters of authorities reported having regular cross-agency or departmental meetings to facilitate the planning of throughcare and aftercare services. Although there did not appear to be many specific throughcare and aftercare planning groups, two authorities mentioned the development of local branches of the national Throughcare Aftercare Forum, which covered several authorities in the area and involved representatives from benefits, housing, careers and health services. We found that in most authorities, throughcare and aftercare planning came under the remit of a range of groups, including children's services planning groups, housing or youth homelessness strategy groups (including a joint throughcare and youth homeless group and a youth housing and aftercare strategy group), SIP meetings, joint committees for children and young people and a corporate parenting working group. Seven authorities (23%) said they did not have any cross-agency meetings for throughcare and aftercare planning.

Working arrangements: agency views

To complement and expand upon the information from the social work departments on corporate and inter-agency partnerships, we sought the views of a number of statutory and voluntary agencies. These were identified during the course of the policy survey.

Just over half (56%) of the 178 agencies that were contacted responded to the questionnaire. Table 7.2 indicates those agencies who were contacted and the number of responses received.

FORMAL AGREEMENTS

All agencies, with the exception of the Children's Reporters Administration and care leavers projects, were asked whether they had formal agreements with the social work department in respect of services for young people who are preparing to leave care or who have left care. We also asked whether they had key members of staff to link with the social work department. Of the 68 responses, we found that just over two-thirds (69%) of the agencies provided specific services to these young people, but only 9 per cent of them reported that formal agreements were in place. The majority (66%) of these agreements were between the social work and housing departments.

Over half of the responding agencies (53%) said they had a member of staff
with responsibility for liaising with the social work department, regarding
throughcare and aftercare services. Link staff were reported in 72 per cent
of the responding housing departments, 71 per cent of the education
departments, 60 per cent of health service providers, 11 per cent of employment services and 38 per cent of the careers companies.

Table 7.2 Supplementary questionnaires sent to other agencies

	Sent out	Received
Housing department	31	18
Other housing providers	5	1
Education department	31	14
Health services	13	5
Employment services	13	9
Careers companies	32	21
Projects for care leavers	16	11
Children's reporters	36	20
Community services	1	0

CROSS-AGENCY/DEPARTMENTAL MEETINGS

Analysis of the Children's Services Plans indicated a strong commitment to
multi-agency collaboration in providing and planning services for looked
after young people and care leavers. This was reflected in our survey of
agencies.

Overall, we found that 70 per cent of the responding agencies were
involved in cross-agency meetings to plan or review throughcare and aftercare services. Careers companies, health service providers, housing departments and education were highly represented with 86 per cent, 80 per cent,
77 per cent and 71 per cent respectively participating in these meetings. A
fifth of responding authority reporters (20%) had been involved in cross-
agency meetings; however, the majority of these consisted of a one-off or
occasional attendance. One children's reporter commented that this was
'not very satisfactory'. All of the responding care leaver projects reported
that they had taken part in cross-agency meetings.

WORKING TOGETHER

Agencies were asked to comment on their current working arrangements with the social work department and rate these arrangements on a five-point scale of 'very good' to 'very poor'. Overall, we found that working arrangements were generally viewed positively, with 13 per cent of responding agencies describing them as 'very good' and 37 per cent describing them as 'good'. Over a quarter (29%) viewed arrangements as 'satisfactory', with over half of the responding careers companies (57%) describing their arrangements as such. However, 14 per cent of agencies indicated that working arrangements with the social work department were less than satisfactory, with 9 per cent describing them as 'poor', 3 per cent describing them as 'very poor' and 2 per cent commenting that arrangements varied from satisfactory to poor. This was particularly so for over a quarter of responding careers companies (29%) and 14 per cent of responding housing departments.

A more detailed consideration of the different agencies' perspectives on working arrangements in respect of throughcare and aftercare was undertaken. As we see from the following comments, this suggested that overall agencies felt that improvements could and should be made in this area.

HOUSING

In respect of housing providers, the majority (61%) thought that working arrangements were more than satisfactory and generally involved good communication and shared goals. However, several commented that although much progress had been made in developing joint working processes, there remained areas of weakness. For example, the exchange of information around client details, the problem of some young people 'slipping through the net', the lack of staff and resources to address policy and procedure deficiencies and the occasional conflict of respective priorities were highlighted.

EDUCATION

Here, working arrangements with the social work department were viewed very positively, with the majority of responding education departments describing them as 'good' (57%) or 'very good' (29%). A small number commented that although links between the departments were good, the area of specific services for looked after young people and care leavers needed to be developed. One education department commented that they had 'good arrangements for mentoring children in care, but no real focus on aftercare'. There was also a recognised need for 'consistent co-ordination' and the availability of 'time and personnel' to strengthen working links.

CAREERS

As the main avenue for providing information and access to employment, training and education for young people, the careers companies have a significant contribution to make to the preparation process and support of care leavers. However, only 5 per cent of responding careers companies reported having formal agreements with the social work department with regards to throughcare and aftercare. The majority (57%) of careers companies described their working arrangements as 'satisfactory'. Most described informal arrangements that were only just beginning to strengthen. However, some dissatisfaction at working arrangements in respect of throughcare and aftercare was expressed by the careers companies. 'Poor' or 'very poor' working arrangements were highlighted in 29 per cent of responses. Areas of concern focused on the ad hoc nature of the contact between the two services. Comments suggested that contact seemed to be dependent on the willingness and knowledge of individual social workers or throughcare workers and could be somewhat one-sided, with the careers companies taking the initiative. One careers respondent reported that:

> We first raised concerns about this issue of joint guidance for young people leaving care in 1995. The recent focus on throughcare and aftercare arrangements has at last led to social work taking notice...although we are still waiting for a formal response.

Nevertheless, there was a significant amount of optimism for future progress contained within the response of the careers companies. Many expressed their commitment to formalising and strengthening their involvement in services for young people who are preparing to leave or had left care. Several pointed towards the introduction of the LAC material as a means of introducing a more systematic, procedural basis for joint working. The recommendations of the Beattie Report were also highlighted as a means of taking this forward.

EMPLOYMENT SERVICE

The majority of responding employment services (55%) described their working arrangements with the social work department as less than satisfactory. It would appear that there was little contact between the two with regards to throughcare and aftercare issues, although it was felt by several of the responding services that stronger links were needed 'to enable smoother transition for care leavers into mainstream services'. In some areas, work to build greater communication and co-operation was underway.

CHILDREN'S REPORTERS

The majority (85%) of responding children's reporters described their current working arrangements with the social work department in respect of throughcare and aftercare as 'good' (70%) or 'very good' (15%). However, within this, it was felt that improved procedures were necessary. The main areas of concern surrounded establishing and adhering to protocols. A number of children's reporters were critical of social work procedures. For example, it was suggested in one case that 'the reporter is often an afterthought', while others felt that it was sometimes difficult to ascertain areas of responsibility and commented that despite agreed structures, social workers did not always 'keep their part of the agreement'. The issue of late reports was also raised. It was generally acknowledged that these issues were in part a consequence of restructuring both within local authorities and the organising of the Children's Reporters Administration. Regular meetings, a 'mutual respect' and understanding of respective roles and involvement on planning committees seemed to be indicative of 'good' working arrangements.

HEALTH SERVICE PROVIDERS

The majority of responding health services (80%) described working arrangements with the social work department as 'good'. However, one commented that this very much depended on goodwill, as there were no formal arrangements between them.

PROJECTS FOR CARE LEAVERS

All but one of the responding projects were positive about their working arrangements with the social work department. Half described them as satisfactory, 30 per cent said they were 'good' and 20 per cent reported 'very good' working arrangements. However, two expressed a desire to see improvements and one commented that 'they're [social work] not in touch with what young people want!' One project, which said that their working arrangements with the social work department were poor, felt that there was often a conflict of interests between themselves and the social work department as their managing agent.

Finally, having looked at support in terms of the inter-agency framework, how did the young people in our three areas experience the range of professional support?

Support from other professionals: young people's experiences
In addition to help from social workers and specialist leaving care workers, young people were asked about other sources of professional support or advice that had helped them since they left care. As Table 7.3 shows, most young people (74%) had been in contact with careers and the Jobcentre (68%). Furthermore, over a quarter of those who had been in contact said that this contact had been very helpful (26% and 30%).

Young people were asked to comment on the help or lack of help they had received from these services. Their experiences illustrate both the variety of need, which is often emotional as well as practical, and what they had found useful.

A number of young people commented on their experience of seeking support on career options. Corrine had left residential care 11 months earlier. At the point of joining the study she was working towards a Scottish vocational qualification (SVQ) in business administration with the help of her ex-residential key worker and the local careers company:

> My careers advisor is very good and listens to what I want to be doing with myself instead of putting me anywhere and that's it. She spoke to me about all different things and found something I really enjoy. I see her every week or two weeks, whatever I can manage.

Alan highlighted the increased access to support that his training placement had brought him:

> Other workers in my placement and in a project which I attend help me to deal with feelings and I'm getting help from my college tutor who will talk to me about anything to do with my course or life.

Deb had experienced some difficulties in finding a career; however, a year on from leaving care she had taken on some voluntary work and had recently started a college course in youth work. She commented:

> Careers weren't listening to me. I changed what I wanted to do but they wouldn't listen so I never went back. CSV [Community Service Volunteers] have been amazing, though, getting me my volunteer placement, encouraging me with college. If I ever need help and support they are there.

Although Deb was doing well with her career, her wider situation highlighted some of the difficulties care leavers experience when trying to manage living independently, particularly if they are unable to access relevant support. Deb was struggling financially and finding it difficult to keep up payments on her flat. Despite seeking help, she told us: 'The

Table 7.3 Contact with other support professionals after leaving care

	No contact (%)	Contact over the follow-up (%)		
		No help	Some help	Very helpful
Voluntary project worker	93	0	4	3
Other service	89	0	5	6
Criminal justice worker	86	2	7	5
Drug/alcohol counsellor	86	6	4	4
Who Cares? Scotland	86	3	5	6
Homelessness officer	82	3	12	4
Health worker	81	1	6	12
Barnardo's worker	79	1	2	18
Housing advisor	73	9	13	5
Employer/training staff	69	5	19	7
Teacher/tutor	65	7	14	14
Benefits advisor	45	13	31	11
Jobcentre	32	18	32	18
Careers advisor	26	11	41	22

Housing [Office], well I just argued with them constantly. They were no help with rent arrears, they couldn't understand the situation I was in.'

As is illustrated by the following comments, there was evidence of a wide range of help to address specific needs as well as more mainstream issues. Again, experiences of accessing support were mixed.

Heather was unemployed at T2. She commented: 'The Jobcentre were no help, they just sent me to the social.' She had, however, received some specific support with her education difficulties: 'My support unit teachers were helpful. They worked with me my way.'

Lucy had received help to deal with her addiction problems and to work towards rebuilding her life:

> The drug counsellor was helpful because it basically got me realising what the stuff was doing to me…helping me to get back on my feet. The Jobcentre helped to get me from the dole to a job. They were always like phoning me up and saying there's a job there and my employer helped me with my wages and stuff.

Finally, Anna had experienced considerable housing difficulties since leaving care. Over the follow-up she and her child had moved six times, mostly from bed and breakfast accommodation to hotels and hostels. She told us, 'The homeless officer just moved us when we complained, didn't try to deal with the complaints and get us extra facilities. I complained about a lack of cooking facilities so she moved us to a hotel with no cooking facilities.' Anna had, however, found the support from her health visitor very helpful. 'My health visitor gave advice and got me access to services for my child that the GP didn't offer.'

Conclusion

Responding to the wide range of needs of care leavers requires corporate parenting – as is recognised under Section 21 of the Children (Scotland) Act. Social workers and leaving care workers may need to draw on the wider range of professional support available. Often this requires them to take on the role of co-ordinating services. Having inter-agency strategies in place can help facilitate this process and ensure that young people are able to receive and make use of the type of services they require, to meet their needs as quickly and smoothly as possible.

Our policy survey provided evidence of strong links with housing but fewer reported links with education, careers, health, benefits agencies and the children's reporter. In addition, good links with voluntary organisations and SIPs existed. Where formal working arrangements were in place they were generally seen by corporate and external agencies as positive. In some cases, however, the development of clearer and stronger inter-agency procedures was required.

Our young people's comments on their own experience of support also showed that they were making use of a wide range of agencies (e.g. careers, benefits and voluntary projects). This demonstrated a wide range of professional input into leaving care support. For some young people, however, the level of assistance did not always live up to their expectations or needs.

Chapter 8

What Makes a Difference? Outcomes for Young People Leaving Care: the Follow-up Study

Introduction

Our preceding chapters have looked at the initial post-care destination of all young people who participated in the study. In this chapter we focus on a sub-group of young people who went on to participate in the follow-up study. We explore some of the general characteristics, experiences and post-care circumstances of this group of care leavers and consider both their initial outcomes at T1 (baseline) and their final outcomes at T2 (six months later).[1]

The main purpose of this section is to look at factors that may contribute to successful transitions from care. While these young people have had a variety of experiences and were at various stages of their transition to independent living, we have been able to identify some of the factors that influence the likelihood of successful and unsuccessful transitions and outcomes. Before doing so, it is worth considering what we mean by outcomes and how we have approached the task of assessing them.

We have adopted the definition of outcomes used by Knapp (1989). Here, outcomes are described as the effects or results of a process. For the purpose of this study the *process* may be seen as a combination of the care experience and the support or intervention young people have received. Because support often serves as a mediator between care experiences and outcomes, we have looked at the two aspects of this process separately; first, in terms of selected elements of the care experience (predictors) and, second, the presence or lack of formal support (intervention). We have also used two sets of outcomes: baseline outcomes at T1 which are in effect the starting points for the follow-up study, and final outcomes at T2 which describe the young person's status at the close of the study.

In terms of assessing outcomes, we have employed bivariate analysis to explore which factors influence outcomes for these young people. A regression analysis was also conducted to identify which factors were most closely associated with key outcome measures, such as accommodation and career outcomes. It is important to note, however, that statistical analysis was ultimately restricted by the small sample size and, to a lesser extent, the short follow-up time span. We have drawn, therefore, on qualitative evidence from selected cases to supplement the statistical findings. The selection of these cases was guided by outcomes at T1 and T2 and young people's progress over the follow-up time span. For example, a proportion of those whose outcomes had improved, remained constant and deteriorated were extracted for qualitative analysis.

Introducing the follow-up group

This chapter concentrates on the follow-up group only. As outlined in Chapter 1, the group comprises those young people who provided information at T1 and who then went on to take part in a second round of data collection six months later at T2 (n=61).

Follow-up information was gathered from most young people 11 months on from leaving care, although it ranged from 5 to 24 months. We also sought information from young people's main support worker (e.g. a leaving care worker or social worker). As we have seen, however, many young people had ended or lost contact with their support workers by T2 and as a result information was received from just over half (58%) of those contacted.

In looking at the general characteristics of the group we found that more young women (59%) than men had taken part in the follow-up study and while 23 per cent of the group came from Shire and 18 per cent from County, the majority (59%) were from City authority. Most (64%) of the group had been looked after away from home in either foster care (28%), residential care (25%) or other care placements, such as relatives and training flats attached to residential units (11%). Just over a third, meanwhile, had been looked after at home (36%). At the point of entry to the study, the majority of the group (56%) had moved to a range of independent or semi-independent accommodation. Just under half (44%) had remained at or returned home after leaving care. We also found that one in ten (10%) young people in the follow-up group were parents at the point of joining the study. This number rose to almost two in ten (18%) over the six-month follow-up. Over half (55%) of these young people were lone parents and most (82%) were caring for their child full-time.

Further details of the follow-up group, such as age of leaving care, educational attainment and heath and well-being issues are discussed in the following sections, where we explore factors that impact upon outcomes.

Analysing outcomes

As outlined above, we have looked at outcomes in terms of certain predictors that may be expected to have some influence upon a young person's life chances after leaving care. We have also considered any support or intervention that may have advanced good predictors or mediated poor predictors. Finally, we have assessed young people's baseline outcomes and final outcomes as a means of charting their progress over the follow-up study.

Predictors

Evidence from existing research has been used to inform the selection of key factors for use in our study. By examining whether or not these factors have an influence on outcomes it may be possible to use them to *predict* whether or not a successful outcome may be achieved or expected.

Young people in the follow-up group were categorised as having a good or a poor predictor across a range of measures. We have used the terms good and poor for the purpose of distinguishing one group from another i.e. it is often the case that young people fall into these groups by being better or worse than each other, and as such the terms should be seen as relative rather than as examples of what would generally be termed good or poor. For the purpose of assessing outcomes within our study, good predictors generally represented protective factors, while poor predictors were seen as risk indicators.

AGE AT LEAVING CARE

The first predictor to be considered was the age at leaving care. As we have seen in earlier chapters, evidence from previous research suggests that young people who leave care early for independent living are accelerated towards adult responsibilities (occupationally, financially and personally) far sooner than their non-looked-after peers. Such young people may face an increased chance of financial hardship, unemployment and homelessness. It is likely therefore that the age at which young people leave or move on from care may have some impact upon future life chances.

Overall, almost three-quarters (72%) of young people in the follow-up group had left care or moved to independent living before the age of 17. In terms of assessing age predictors, those who had moved on from care before the age of 17 were categorised as having a 'poor' age predictor (72%) while those who had moved on from care at 17 or over were categorised as having a 'good' age predictor (28%).

PLACEMENT MOVEMENT

Movement in care can lead to disruption in a young person's personal, emotional and educational development. Research indicates that frequent placement moves may result in difficulties in forming attachments, poor educational attainment and subsequently an increased likelihood of unemployment and social exclusion. Stability of care placement is therefore important for establishing continuity of care and promoting positive life chances.

Almost a quarter (24%) of young people in the follow-up study had experienced four or more placement moves during their last care episode. The average number of placement moves for the group, however, was two. Those who had experienced more moves than average (three or more) were categorised as having a poor placement stability predictor (32%) and those with the average number of moves or less (up to two) were described as having a good predictor (68%).

SCHOOL NON-ATTENDANCE

Young people who miss school either through exclusion or truancy are at greater risk of leaving school early and doing so with fewer qualifications. This can have far-reaching consequences in terms of employment, financial independence and stable accommodation arrangements.

Over two-thirds of our follow-up group had been excluded from school. These young people were categorised as having a poor predictor (68%). Those who had not been excluded were assigned a good predictor (32%).

Truancy was also very common within the group; however, some degree of truancy is perhaps usual. Truancy predictors were therefore constructed to take account of this. Those young people who said they had never truanted (15%) or had done so occasionally (33%) were categorised as having a good predictor while those who had truanted often (52%) had a poor predictor.

DIFFICULTIES

Some young people in the follow-up group had experienced difficulties both during and since leaving care. While the presence of early difficulties may act as a risk indicator for poor outcomes on leaving care, any difficulties experienced after care can destabilise a young person's coping mechanisms and undermine or impede good outcomes and positive progress. It is important, therefore, to consider the presence and possible effects of difficulties when assessing outcomes and progress in wider life areas.

As discussed in earlier chapters, mental health and emotional and behavioural problems are evident amongst the care leaver population. A measure of these difficulties within the follow-up group was based upon the support worker's rating of the extent to which such difficulties were present in a young person's life at both baseline and the follow-up stage. Almost two-thirds (62%) of the group were rated as having mild to severe difficulties with mental health or emotional and behavioural problems, indicating some risk. Over a third (38%) had no difficulties in this area.

Having difficulties with substance misuse was another risk indicator. This measure was based upon whether a young person reported having had problems with alcohol, drugs or solvents since leaving care. The majority (80%) of the group did not report a problem in this area; however, one in five (20%) young people said they had experienced difficulties with one or more of these issues.

A measure of problems associated with offending was also developed. This was based upon young people's reports of having committed an offence or being cautioned or convicted of an offence. Most (77%) said that this had not been an issue either currently or in the past, while almost a quarter (23%) reported some involvement with offending.

FAMILY LINKS

Finally, a measure of support from family during and after care was constructed. Previous research indicates that good family links and support can lead to positive outcomes. Family links are important for practical help, such as help with accommodation and finding work, financial assistance and emotional support. Biehal et al. (1995) also found that it promoted more competent relationship skills.

Good and poor predictors were determined on the basis of a young person's contact with their birth family and whether or not they considered this contact helpful. For example, those who described their contact with a family member as sometimes or mostly helpful were categorised as having a good predictor (86%), and those who had no contact or had unhelpful contact were categorised as having a poor predictor (14%).

Each of the key predictors outlined above were used in statistical analysis as a means of exploring their impact upon outcomes and progress. Where statistical associations were found, we have reported our finding within the discussion of outcomes later in the chapter. Predictors were also considered qualitatively as an aid to making sense of young people's experiences and outcomes and any positive or negative changes in their progress over the follow-up period.

Intervention: throughcare and aftercare support

The second issue likely to have an impact upon outcomes for young people leaving care is the throughcare and aftercare support they have received. As we have seen, a significant number of young people in the follow-up group had poor predictors in one or more key areas. A central aim of leaving care support is to help mediate these factors and assist young people towards achieving positive outcomes, whatever their early experience or starting points may be.

An indication of throughcare support was derived from asking support workers whether or not a young person had received a planned programme of preparation. Less than a third (28%) of young people in the follow-up study had. Over half (56%) had not received a planned programme and in 16% of cases the worker was either unsure or had not provided information.

Support (or intervention) from social workers and leaving care workers after care was assessed in terms of their contact with a young person at T1 and T2. Table 8.1 indicates the presence of support.

Table 8.1 Percentage of young people who had contact with support workers at T1 and T2

	Social worker (%)	Leaving care worker (%)	Both (%)	No contact with either (%)
T1	38	34	16	43
T2	29	44	20	44
T1 and T2	20	31	7	38

As discussed in previous chapters, the provision of aftercare support was strongly linked to whether or not a young person was looked after away from home. In terms of the follow-up group, we found a highly significant association at T1 and T2 between the presence of support from either a social worker ($p<0.001$; $p=0.004$) or a leaving care worker ($p<0.001$; $p=0.001$) and whether the young person had been looked after at home or away from home in foster or residential care. Figure 8.1 illustrates the difference in levels of support for the two groups.

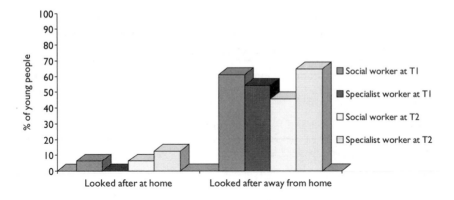

Figure 8.1 Support at T1 and T2 for young people looked after at home and away from home

Overall, almost two-thirds (62%) of the follow-up group had received some form of intervention since leaving care, although for 8 per cent this had involved limited contact only (such as contact with either a specialist leaving care worker or a social worker at T1 or T2 only). Over a third (38%) of the group, however, had not received any intervention.

In addition to looking at the presence of support we also explored the quality of support. For this purpose, an overall measure of support was constructed. This involved combining the measure of contact with support workers over the follow-up period and young people's perceptions of how helpful it had been. Good support involved having contact with a support worker and finding the contact mostly or very helpful. Poor support was not having contact with a support worker or having unhelpful contact. This was in turn combined to give a three-point measure of the level of support at baseline and over the six-month follow-up. Those who had good support from a social worker and a leaving care worker were rated as having a high level of support while those who had good support from at least one worker were rated as having a medium level of support. Young people who had poor support from both support workers or from their only support worker and those without support were rated as having low-level or no support. Table 8.2 gives a breakdown of support for young people at baseline and over the follow-up period.

Measures of intervention were used in both statistical and qualitative analysis to explore any impact upon final outcomes.

Table 8.2 Support from social worker
and specialist leaving care worker

	Social worker (%)		Specialist leaving care worker (%)		Level of overall support (%)		
	Good	Poor	Good	Poor	High	Medium	Low/none
Baseline	25	61*	33*	56*	16	25	59
Follow-up	21	72*	44	56*	15	36	49

*Some young people responded 'unsure'

Assessing outcomes: what makes a difference?

In this section we look at the range of factors that may have influenced baseline and final outcomes. This involves bringing together predictors and intervention to examine their influence on both sets of outcomes. Outcomes at baseline are in effect starting points for the follow-up study and as such were also measured against final outcomes.[2] This enabled us to chart the direction of progress over the follow-up period. This assessment of progress (e.g. improved, deteriorated, etc.) in each of the outcome areas was in turn considered in terms of predictors and intervention to provide an indication of what factors make a difference in promoting positive outcomes and progress. Qualitative information gathered from interviews with young people was used to illustrate individual and general experiences. The case illustrations present examples of those who had good or poor outcomes and had improved or deteriorated over the follow-up.

The outcomes areas measured included life skills, family and social networks and the key areas of accommodation and career. Outcome areas were measured across a good/poor or good/fair/poor dimension and were based mainly on information supplied by young people. However, support workers' perceptions, where available, were used to inform the overall decision.

Life skills: preparation and coping

Our first outcome area is how well a young person was managing with life after leaving care. As an indication of a young person's life skills we looked at how well prepared they felt at baseline and how well they felt they were coping at the follow-up stage in a range of life skills areas. These included self-care and practical skills (healthy eating, personal care, cooking, cleaning, shopping and budgeting), relationship skills (informal, formal and sexual) and well-being and lifestyle (hobbies, awareness of safe sex practices and issues related to alcohol and drugs). Two scales were constructed, the first to explore the adequacy of preparation and the second to explore how well young people felt they were managing in these life skill areas.

Reliability analysis was carried out on each scale to establish the level of confluence amongst the items within the scales. Results indicated that items worked sufficiently well to allow us to calculate an overall score for each scale by summing the scores of each item.[3] This enabled us to construct an indication of starting points (preparation) and outcomes (coping) in terms of life skills.

PREPARATION

The preparation scale consisted of 13 items. Scores for preparation were reversed so those with lower scores in fact reported having had more preparation. The average score for the group was 8 out of a possible score of 39. Good outcomes were assigned to those who had better than average scores (1–7) and poor outcomes were given for those scoring 8 or above (see Figure 8.2).

For exploratory purposes a factor analysis of the items in the preparation scale was carried out. This suggested a number of possible models, one of which enabled us to construct the following preparation sub-scales by summing the scores of relevant items:[4]

- self-care scale (skin and hair care, healthy eating, keeping fit)
- social life scale (hobbies, socialising, boy- and girlfriends)
- domestic scale (cooking, shopping, budgeting)
- lifestyle scale (safe sex, alcohol, drugs, smoking).

COPING SKILLS

The coping scale consisted of 12 items. Coping was scored out of a possible 36: the higher the score, the better the young person's perception of their ability to cope in life skills areas at T2. Good outcomes were assigned to those scoring 25 or more and poor outcomes indicated a score of 24 or less (see Figure 8.2).

Workers' perceptions of life skills were also sought; however, information from this source was not available for all cases. Where information was available there was a general consensus between young people's and workers' perception of coping with life skills.

A factor analysis of the items was also conducted on this scale, using several different rotation models and extraction criteria. Two clear coping sub-scales were suggested:[5]

- Housekeeping scale (able to clean home, able to do laundry, able to shop for food and other things, and able to budget). It is notable that the item relating to ability to cook for oneself did not fit well in this factor.

- Health and social life scale (able to make friends, able to eat healthily, able to follow hobbies and interests, able to keep fit).

As Figure 8.2 shows, over half of the young people in the follow-up group felt that they had received adequate preparation for adult life and a similar number felt that they were coping well with these responsibilities at T2.

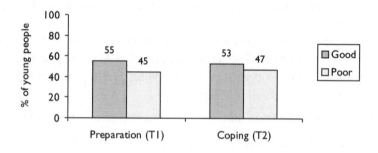

Figure 8.2 Life skills outcomes

What makes a difference to life skills?

Analysis of the preparation and coping scales indicated a statistical link between these two scales and also in relation to gender. Correlations were calculated between each of the preparation sub-scales and the overall scale, and with the sub-scales relating to coping outcomes. Both the 'domestic' and 'lifestyle' preparation scales were significantly correlated with the overall coping outcome scale ($p=0.010$ and $p=0.045$ respectively). However, in addition, the 'social life' preparation scale was significantly correlated with the 'health and social life' coping sub-scale.

In terms of gender differences, there was a significant difference in the 'domestic' preparation sub-scales where females felt significantly better prepared ($p=0.018$).

Analysis of the coping outcome scale also revealed a statistically significant gender difference in coping in life skills areas, with females tending to do better than males. Importantly, we also found a strong statistical link between overall preparation for leaving care (young people's and worker's assessments) and young people's ability to cope at T2.

The two coping sub-scales were helpful in learning more about these relationships. Looking first at the gender differences, there was a significant difference in the 'housekeeping' sub-scale with females coping better than males (p=0.002). There was also some indication that males coped slightly better in the 'health and social life' sub-scale, but not significantly so.

Looking at young people's self-assessment of preparation for leaving care, there was a significant positive correlation between the preparation score and the 'health and social life' coping score[6] but not between preparation and coping with 'housekeeping'.

In summary, these findings suggest that there is evidence that preparation is significantly related to coping in some areas. Preparation in terms of domestic tasks and lifestyle (information on safe sex and substance misuse, etc.) appears to be the most important in terms of overall coping, although preparation in terms of social skills can also enhance social coping. There was also a gender dimension to preparation and coping, although as we have seen this tended to be along the lines of gender-stereotyped roles with females feeling much better prepared for domestic tasks and hence feeling that they were coping better at T2.

Furthermore, in the course of analysis we found no difference between those young people who had been looked after at home and those who had been looked after away from home, either in terms of outcomes for preparation or coping. This suggests that preparation undertaken by substitute carers or leaving care workers was just as effective as that provided by parents and family.

Preparation is clearly a crucial factor in providing a basis for coping with adult life for all young people whether looked after at home or away from home. At a broader level, however, there was some evidence that difficulties such as offending and substance misuse could weaken young people's ability to develop competent life skills. For example, almost all (92%) of those who had poor life skills had experienced problems related to offending (p=0.012) while those who had problems with substance misuse were far more likely to have poor life skills when compared to those who did not report such problems (81% compared to 31%; p=0.001).

There were many indications of good preparation and ongoing support to cope after care from carers, social workers and leaving care services. One of the better examples is illustrated by Mike, a young care leaver who, despite having poor outcomes for family links, had reported good outcomes for both preparation and coping. The determining factors in this case included being looked after in stable long-term foster care until the age of 18 and receiving good support during and after the time he was looked after. Although Mike had not received a planned programme of preparation, he felt that he had been provided with enough support and information in all preparation areas, except for budgeting, in which he reported having had some support. He considered his foster carers and social worker to have offered most help in terms of preparation skills, although friends had been of some help. During the follow-up stage this young person had been resident in a homeless hostel for a short while before moving to a furnished tenancy with support provided by the specialist leaving care scheme. He continued to see his ex-foster carers on a regular basis, which he found 'helpful' and hoped would continue. In addition to continuing support from his ex-carers, this young person also received a well-rounded package of support covering accommodation, employment, emotional and practical support. When asked whether he had received any support in coping with life skills since leaving care he told us: 'My housing development worker helped me to move into my tenancy after she helped me to apply for it and my support worker helped me with benefits as well as homemaking and housekeeping skills which is ongoing.'

Overall, this young person felt well supported and was able to look at his experience of care in a positive light. In terms of the overall effects of being in care he told us, 'It helped me to grow up and help me achieve more than if I had not been in care.'

While over a third (37%) of the young people in the follow-up group had good preparation and coping outcomes at T1 and T2, a fifth had poor outcomes throughout. Factors common to those with poor outcomes included a lack of support during the preparation stage. This involved having not received a planned programme of preparation or reporting a lack of information and support in preparation areas. For some, this had not been redressed after leaving care.

For Nicola, a young woman who had poor outcomes in both preparation and in coping, a combination of poor predictors, chaotic home life and a lack of intervention were apparent. Having experienced two placement moves during her last year of being accommodated, this young woman had left foster care at 16 to return to an unsuitable home environment. Her early departure from care and refusal to engage with support meant that she had not received a planned programme of preparation, and while some basic preparation had been undertaken by her foster carers, she felt that she had not received enough support or information in any of the life skill areas.

Although Nicola had remained at home throughout the follow-up period she was unhappy and had resorted to alcohol and drugs, which were available in the household, to deal with the situation. She commented on the lack of intervention from social work and leaving care services and clearly felt unsupported since returning home. While some of her coping skills may have been mediated by her mother, who carried out most of the household chores, the young person was clearly not coping well. Since returning home her health had suffered as a consequence of her lifestyle and in addition to substance misuse she had developed poor eating habits: 'I don't eat meals, just snacks and crisps. I used to eat meals at foster parents but not so much at home 'coz I'm rubbish at cooking.'

For a small number of young people, there was evidence of a deterioration in life skills outcomes over the follow-up period. Over a tenth (16%) of young people who had reported receiving adequate preparation at T1 had gone on to achieve poor coping outcomes at T2. It would appear that in several cases the good preparation undertaken by family, carers or social workers had been undermined by the difficult circumstances in which young people had found themselves after leaving care. We found examples of this both for young people who were receiving ongoing specialist support and those who had received no intervention throughout the follow-up period. For example, Una, who was receiving an intensive package of specialist support, was failing to cope with the responsibilities of adult life, both in terms of life skills and wider issues, such as maintaining a tenancy. Having left foster care at 16 after four placement moves, this young person had been unable to sustain a number of tenancies due to her chaotic lifestyle. This had involved drug use, offending and allowing friends to overrun her flat. Despite these difficulties, she was confident that with support things were getting better:

> [After] two months I still live in the same tenancy. I have had help from my support worker to keep my flat as well as I do and I have had loads of help from him to sort out my benefits. I have learned my lesson and don't make mistakes I made by letting too many people stay in my flat.

Another young woman, Rona, had returned home from foster care just after her 16th birthday and had taken on the role of caring for her disabled mother. Although she felt that she had received adequate preparation, mostly from family and her social worker, she found that her coping skills were being challenged by the level of responsibility she had acquired since returning home:

> I have to do everything in the house. I don't mind but it can all be a bit too much, especially when I could be looking after myself in my own house.

> Don't get me wrong, I love my mum and don't mind helping, but it does get a bit too much eventually.

Although this young person was receiving a care allowance for looking after her mother, there was no evidence of professional support throughout the follow-up period. As a care leaver returning home she was not a priority for specialist services and although her social worker told us that some informal contact had been maintained initially, she added, 'sadly, existing caseloads mean that it's not possible to keep up to date in closed cases'.

In terms of making progress in life skills areas, just under a fifth (16%) of young people had improved on their poor outcome at T1 and had reported good coping skills at T2. While continuing intervention and post-care stability were apparent in some cases, for others good support, family links and a positive 'role model' had been important factors. For example, Heather had moved on from being looked after at home to her own tenancy with a partner. Despite feeling that she had not had enough support or information in most life areas and having gone through a 'wild child phase', she was now settling down to independent living, with ongoing support from her family. When asked how she was coping, Heather commented:

> ...better than expected. I was worried, money wise, whether I would get to see mum regularly [but] I'm getting the hang of it now. I find myself coming in at a reasonable time, the time my mum wanted me to come in, and eating the things my mum used to try and get me to eat. It's funny how things work out.

Having support from family, as in Heather's case, or from a partner or friends was an important factor in helping many young people cope with independent living. This highlights the importance of encouraging and facilitating ongoing contact with family and wider social ties while young people are looked after.

Family links and social networks

Our second outcome area is family and social networks. Developing and maintaining contact with family and social networks were important in terms of general outcomes as well as sources of support. Two outcome measures for exploring contact and support from family and friends were used.

FAMILY LINKS

Good outcomes involved having contact with a family member and describing that contact as sometimes or mostly helpful. Poor outcomes included having no contact or contact that was considered by the young person as unhelpful.

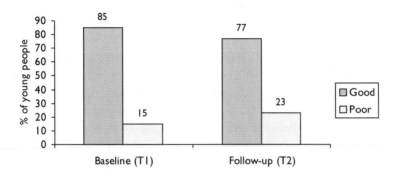

Figure 8.3 Family links outcomes

While there was a slight deterioration in family contact by T2, most (84%) young people had maintained good links throughout the follow-up period. As discussed in earlier sections, positive family links are an important factor in establishing a system of support for young people making the transition to adulthood. For most young people in the follow-up sample, families appeared to be providing emotional and practical support in most life areas. Young people were able to rely on family for help with money, food, advice, help with finding work and also with finding or providing accommodation, whether long term or in times of need. Family support came from extended family as well as immediate family members, particularly in cases where relationships with parents had broken down. Although mothers were most commonly cited as the person to whom young people would turn if in need of help, siblings, grandparents and aunts were also identified as important sources of emotional support and, in some cases, accommodation.

Around three-quarters of young people who were looked after away from home had good family links at T1 and T2 (79% and 75% respectively). This suggested that, for most, family links had been encouraged during the time that they had been accommodated.

WHAT MAKES A DIFFERENCE TO FAMILY LINKS?
Information from young people and workers about the provision of support to maintain links or reconcile differences with family was limited. However, examples of support included financing or providing transport to and from the family home, arranging visits and overnight stays to facilitate reintegra-

tion into the family unit and mediating family contact. For example, Cathy had been looked after in children's homes and foster care on and off since the age of 11. She had good family outcomes throughout the follow-up period due to the support she had received from her grandfather, to whom she felt very close. She told us: 'My grandad helps me by buying clothes and food. I like to be with him, it makes me feel good.' However, at the point of entering the study, Cathy's relationship with her mother was problematic. Home visits had been introduced prior to her discharge from care to prepare her for her return home. Subsequently, her relationship with her mother became strained and her family placement broke down. She returned to foster care briefly before moving to independent living at 16. Cathy was receiving support from the leaving care team and support staff from a young offenders' programme throughout the follow-up period. As part of her support package both teams worked with Cathy to resolve family issues and maintain the supportive links she had with her grandad. This included help with working through difficulties with her mother and transport to visit her grandad. By T2 Cathy had been forced to leave her tenancy due to problems related to drug abuse; however, she had been able to return to live with her mother where she is continuing to receive support with family issues.

Almost a quarter of young people in the follow-up group reported having poor family links at T2. Some had experienced a deterioration of contact during the follow-up period (14% of young people who had been looked after at home and 15% of those who had been looked after away from home) while others had not had contact with family members for some time. Several young people told us that it was their choice not to have contact and therefore they had not wished support with this issue.

For the relatively small proportion who had poor family links at T2 there seemed little evidence that this had affected outcomes in other areas. This was particularly so for those looked after away from home. For example, almost two-thirds (63%) of these young people had achieved positive outcomes in coping with life skills, 70 per cent had good accommodation outcomes and most (90%) had achieved educational qualifications. However, crucially, all of these young people continued to receive a high level of intervention from leaving care workers, social workers or both. This suggests that the effects of poor family links may be mediated by good, consistent aftercare support.

In some cases a stable environment during or after care had also served to redress the lack of family support. For example, Alice had been looked after in children's homes until she moved to supported lodgings at 16. At the point of joining the study she had not had family contact for over two years. Alice told us that it had been her decision to break ties with all family members: 'I didn't want contact, I just left it at that.' Alice had been supported in this decision by her leaving care worker, who helped her to adjust to the loss of family links and to develop her relationship skills by broadening her friendship network. At T2 Alice had achieved a good outcome in terms of social networks and support and had a group of friends who she felt she could rely on for advice and support. Alice was also supported by her supported carers, who she also referred to as her parents. She told us:

> It's just like my family, basically. I interact with the rest of their family as well, they help me with everything, they show me how to budget and show me how to shop, just what normal parents do with their kids, basically.

Despite having poor predictors in terms of placement moves in care (four moves) and educational attainment (no standard grades), by T2 Alice was doing well in all outcome areas. She had achieved a number of qualifications at college, including an Scottish Qualifications Authority (SQA) award in communications and computing and a certificate in travel and tourism, and was managing well with life skills in a stable home environment in which she was being supported in her transition to adult living. Support from leaving care services was ongoing but her worker commented that Alice felt ready to become more independent: 'She is currently deciding which services she no longer needs, which I see as a reflection of her advancing maturity.'

For young people who had been looked after at home and had poor family outcomes, two-thirds (66%) had good coping skills and most (75%) had good or fair accommodation outcomes. While none of the looked after at home group were receiving intervention at T2, they had in common a good network of support from friends and partners.

SOCIAL NETWORKS AND ISOLATION

Grading outcomes for social networks at T1 and T2 took into account young people's reports of contact with friends, whether they had someone to talk to if they felt sad or depressed and the extent to which they experienced loneliness.

A good outcome was achieved if a combination of the above factors suggested that the young person had a support network and rarely if ever felt lonely. A fair outcome was given where factors suggested that a young person was either without close friends or someone to talk to and occasionally felt lonely. A poor outcome indicated a lack of friends and support network, particularly if loneliness was also apparent.

For most, social support outcomes remained constant over the follow-up period. At T1, however, we found that slightly more of those looked after away from home had poor outcomes (15% compared to 9% of those living at home). This appeared to reflect the issue of isolation for those who were living independently.

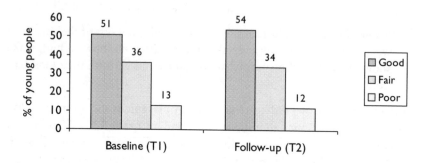

Figure 8.4 Social network outcomes

WHAT MAKES A DIFFERENCE TO SOCIAL SUPPORT?

Most young people felt that they could rely on friends for support; however, it was difficult to determine what had helped these young people to develop or maintain social networks, particularly as many had not received through-care or aftercare support to pursue hobbies or interests. Some exploration of the general characteristics of those who had poor outcomes in social networks revealed that all had good outcomes in terms of family links and most appeared to be able to rely on them for support and advice. Also, all but one had achieved good or fair housing outcomes. There were less positive outcomes in terms of career where all but one of those with poor social networks were unemployed. This latter point raises the importance of participation in education, training and work as a means of broadening social networks and support.

An indication of the impact of poor social networks and isolation was provided by Lee, a young man who had been looked after at home. Lee reported having a good supportive relationship with his family, including step-parents and grandparents; however, at both baseline and follow-up he reported having no real friends:

I am 16 and have no friends. I would love to go out and about with girls and have boy pals but I have no one except my younger brother, but his pals don't like me very much because of what happened in the past. I always feel unsafe and very lonely. I have no confidence and no friends.

Lee felt that his mum had been his main source of support both during the time he was looked after and since his supervision order had ended:

Mum tries to show me how to budget my money; [she] deals with anything that I don't feel I can, but she makes sure that I am comfortable around people and places before she leaves me to deal with things.

He told us that he had felt particularly unsupported by his social worker: 'I felt abandoned when the supervision order was removed. I also had no contact with social services.'

For some young people, lacking a network of social support also had consequences for self-esteem and well-being and coping. All those who had poor social networks also had poor outcomes in coping with life skills, despite almost all having reported good preparation. These young people were also more likely to report negative emotions when asked to rate how they had been feeling. Most (86%) said they felt unhappy sometimes or most of the time and over a third (43%) said they hardly ever or never felt loved. Also, over half (57%) said they hardly ever felt confident and a similar amount said they hardly ever or never felt clever. All except one said that they had often felt confused and angry.

Low self-esteem and confidence and feelings of social isolation are clearly connected. Often they perpetuate one another, with low self-esteem and confidence affecting one's abilities to make and sustain relationships and social isolation affecting one's self-concept. Support and assistance to build social networks can often help to break this cycle.

Only two of those young people who had poor social networks had been offered support with developing relationship skills or broadening friendship networks by their social worker or leaving care worker. A similar number had been helped to pursue hobbies and interests; however, only those looked after away from home and receiving continuing intervention were being supported with these issues.

Accommodation
One of the key outcome areas for young people leaving care is finding suitable post-care accommodation. In order to explore housing issues and progress over the follow-up period, three accommodation measures were constructed and assessed.

COPING

At baseline, accommodation coping outcomes were measured by the support worker's perception of how well the young person was managing in their accommodation. A good outcome was assigned to those rated as managing well or very well (51%) while a poor outcome included managing not so well or not at all well (18%).[7]

Final outcomes for coping with accommodation were based on young people's views on how well they felt able to manage in their accommodation at T2 and whether they were experiencing any problems. Good outcomes included managing well or very well, with no real problems (67%) and poor outcomes included not managing well or experiencing significant problems (33%).

HOUSING MOBILITY

Stability in post-care living was also explored. The number of housing moves during the follow-up period was considered as an indication of the young person's ability to sustain accommodation. Those who had experienced two or more moves (subsequent to their move from care) during the six-month follow-up were assessed as having an unstable housing career (26%) while those who had not moved or had done so only once (74%) were considered to have had a stable housing career.

HOUSING OUTCOMES

Decisions on housing outcomes were based on a combination of factual information (such as the type of accommodation) and whether the young person considered it satisfactory (i.e. they liked living there some or all of the time). Where available, the worker's perception of whether or not the accommodation was suitable for the young person was also taken into account.

Good outcomes generally included supported accommodation, a permanent tenancy, staying with relatives through choice or transitional accommodation that was considered as satisfactory and suitable.

Poor outcomes generally included homelessness and less secure accommodation, such as bed and breakfasts, staying with friends or relatives out of necessity and any type of accommodation in which the young person was unhappy or that was considered unsuitable.

As Figure 8.5 shows, over half of the follow-up group had a good housing outcome at both points in time. An assessment of final housing outcomes revealed some change in the overall picture by T2 with a slight decrease in the number of young people who were rated as having a poor outcome, while the proportion achieving a fair final outcome rose to 31 per cent.

WHAT MAKES A DIFFERENCE TO HOUSING OUTCOMES?
Analysis of housing progress showed that a fifth (20%) of young people had improved their housing outcomes by T2, although for a similar proportion (18%) housing outcomes had deteriorated. In the majority (62%) of cases housing outcomes had remained constant over the six months (either consistently good or poor), regardless of how often a young person had moved.

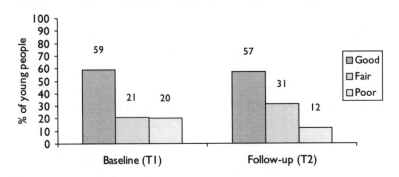

Figure 8.5 Housing outcomes

Almost half (46%) of young people had experienced between one and six moves during the six-month follow-up period and there was an emerging pattern of movement away from family, friends and transitional accommodation towards living either with a partner or alone in a tenancy. In the case of the latter, the percentage of young people living in this type of accommodation had almost doubled. The majority of young people living in the family home were those who had been looked after on a home supervision requirement and it would appear that most had remained in the family home over the follow-up period. A similar pattern emerged when we focused on the housing careers of young people looked after away from home. A movement away from transitional accommodation towards a potentially more secure housing situation was still evident; however, the numbers living in insecure accommodation (for example, with friends or in bed-sits and bed and breakfasts) remained constant over the six-month period. In addition, homelessness had been a problem for around 34 per cent of the follow-up group since leaving care.

Housing mobility did not appear to affect overall housing outcomes. Statistical analysis indicated that there was no difference in the housing outcomes of those who had a stable housing career and those who had moved often during the follow-up period. This suggests that even for those who had an unstable housing career, movement generally resulted in a positive outcome. Achieving successful housing outcomes may be seen as a reflection of the emphasis placed upon accommodation by throughcare and aftercare services, and their ability to act quickly to housing crisis. Certainly, most (75%) young people who had an unstable housing career were receiving ongoing intervention and, statistically, those with higher levels of housing movement tended to be in receipt of higher levels of support from support workers over the six-month follow-up (p=0.029).

A further issue that appeared to have little impact upon overall housing outcomes was young people's care experiences. For example, statistically there was no difference in housing outcomes amongst those who had been looked after at home and those looked after away from home. Also, for young people looked after away from home, there did not appear to be any association between housing outcomes and placement movement while in care. In addition, we found no apparent association between the age of leaving care and young people's perception of how well they were managing with their accommodation at T2 or their overall housing outcomes. Again, this may reflect the ability of throughcare and aftercare support to mediate between early difficulties and subsequent housing outcomes.

An element of young people's experience that did appear to show a significant association with housing outcomes, however, was truancy (p=0.041). Here analysis suggested that those with a poor housing outcome were more likely to have truanted often. Truancy appeared to be a significant risk indicator across a range of areas. Indeed, those young people who had truanted appeared to lead more troubled lives in general, which may in turn have impacted upon their ability to settle into accommodation. For example, we found a statistical association between truancy and difficulties with offending (p=0.013) and substance misuse (p=0.045). Almost all (91%) young people who reported truanting often also reported involvement with offending and the majority (75%) of those who reported difficulties with alcohol, drugs or solvent use had truanted often.

Other factors which influenced final housing outcomes included housing starting points (p<0.001). Over three-quarters (78%) of those who had good housing starting points had also achieved good final outcomes compared to only 28 per cent of those who had poor starting points. This suggested that those who failed to secure good housing arrangements early on tended to fare worse over the follow-up period. There was also some evidence to suggest that good housing outcomes at T2 were associated with accommodation coping skills (p=0.001). Most (61%) of those who were described by their worker as managing well at T1 and the majority (71%) of those who felt they were managing well with their accommodation at T2 had achieved good overall housing outcomes. Those who felt they were not managing well, meanwhile, tended to have poor housing outcomes. Although by no means a straightforward issue, as being unhappy with accommodation is likely to mean that one feels less able to cope with it, this nevertheless suggests that living in unsuitable, poor or unsatisfactory accommodation can undermine or limit a young person's coping skills. This may in turn result in their inability to sustain their accommodation.

There was also evidence to suggest that poor family support over the follow-up period was associated with good housing outcomes (p=0.034). While at first glance this may appear surprising, further examination showed that this may be explained in terms of higher levels of professional intervention for those who were lacking support from family. In fact, all young people with poor family support over the follow-up were receiving ongoing specialist support or support from a social worker at T2.

Generally, it would seem that housing outcomes tended to be most closely linked to aftercare support. That key aspects of the care experience and post-care homelessness and housing instability had little impact on overall housing outcomes indicated that effective aftercare support can mediate between risk factors or difficulties and overall outcomes in this area.

An exploration of young people's views and accounts of accommodation issues offered some indication of what they found helpful. Just under half (46%) had good accommodation at T1 and T2. These young people appeared to have benefited from formal and informal support or a combination of both.

Annie, for example, lived with a supported carer and received ongoing support from a leaving care worker. She also had a long-term boyfriend and said that she would turn to either her support worker or boyfriend to help her if she were in difficulties.

Jim was also supported by a leaving care worker over the follow-up study and had remained in contact with workers from his children's home. He also had good links with his immediate family and at the end of the study he had moved into his own flat with his partner. Jim was full of praise for the help he had received from his support worker: 'He has helped me with everything...if he was not there I don't know how I would have managed.'

All these young people had experienced some changes in their accommodation since leaving care. But what was significant was that there was someone who was able to assist them and help them move onto new accommodation and support them in maintaining themselves.

Young people who had improved their accommodation outcomes from poor starting points benefited in the main from formal support. Alex, for example, had eight house moves in 14 months. He had not had contact with his foster carers since leaving care at 16 and had lived in a number of different types of accommodation over the follow-up study, including bed and breakfasts, returning to his mum, then his dad, and living with friends – all had broken down. He arrived homeless in Shire authority and was assisted by the leaving care team who arranged supported lodgings and have provided ongoing personal support to help him settle in.

Leaving care workers also assisted Jenny, a single parent. After several accommodation breakdowns, intensive work to rebuild family links facilitated her move back to her parents.

Young people whose accommodation outcomes had deteriorated during the two points in time (18%) included two young people on home supervision whose relationships with their parents were very difficult – they both wanted to live elsewhere. In Jan's case there was no social work support at all. In contrast, Sue was receiving a lot of help from specialist leaving care workers and had secured arrangements to move on to her own flat.

Young people also regarded their accommodation as deteriorating if they were living away from close friends, in run-down neighbourhoods or bed and breakfast accommodation.

Less than a tenth (6%) of young people had poor outcomes at both T1 and T2. One young person had no formal support. Liz, who was on home supervision, received no social work contact after her supervision requirement ended, even though her relationship with her mother was very difficult and had broken down on three occasions, resulting in her being homeless each time.

A second young person had no contact at all with his family. He had been homeless on several occasions but had received some help from workers from the homeless unit.

A third young person, Sam, had moved 10 times in the 14 months since leaving care and was homeless at T2. He had not had contact with his social worker since leaving care, but had been returned to leaving care services since becoming homeless and was being assisted by a leaving care worker to find accommodation.

Education and career
The final key outcome area to be explored was education and career.

EDUCATIONAL ATTAINMENT
In terms of education, young people's attainment was assessed according to the number of standard grades they had achieved on leaving care. The average for young people in the general population, of seven standard grades, was used to categorise outcomes.

Good outcomes were assigned to those gaining seven or more standard grades (13%) and fair outcomes were given to young people achieving one to six standard grades (35%). Those who had not achieved any standard grades (52%) were rated as having a poor educational outcome.

EMPLOYMENT AND CAREER PATHS
Employment outcomes for young people at baseline and follow-up were categorised according to the nature of their occupational status.

Good outcomes included employment, education or training and voluntary work if undertaken in addition to either work or education. Poor outcomes included unemployment and voluntary work. Young people who were caring for their child were not included in the outcome categories for employment.

As indicated in Figure 8.6, almost two-thirds of the group had poor outcomes at both points in time, although there was a slight increase in the overall number of young people achieving good outcomes at follow-up. Six months offers limited scope for any real change and indeed, for the majority (74%) of young people in the sample, occupational outcomes remained

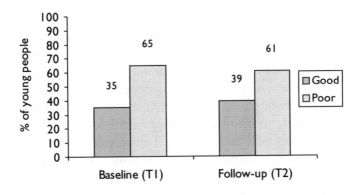

Figure 8.6 Career outcomes

constant over the six-month follow-up period. Unfortunately, two-thirds of these had poor outcomes throughout. There was, however, some degree of movement between career status groups over the follow-up with around one in ten (11%) experiencing a deterioration in their career situation. Slightly more (15%) young people, meanwhile, had improved outcomes at T2 with 8 per cent moving from unemployment to paid work and 7 per cent entering education or training.

WHAT MAKES A DIFFERENCE IN EDUCATION AND CAREER OUTCOMES?

A common characteristic amongst those who had poor educational outcomes was school disruption. Over two-thirds (69%), for example, had truanted often and almost all (91%) of those young people who had experienced exclusion from school had achieved less than average educational attainment (e.g. 32% had fair and 59% had poor educational outcomes). Over half (57%) of those who had good outcomes, meanwhile, had never been excluded.

A second factor common to those who achieved good educational outcomes was stability while in care. All young people with seven or more standard grades had a good placement move predictor which indicates fewer placement moves during their last care episode.

In terms of career status, there did not appear to be any conclusive patterns within the care experience between those achieving better or worse career outcomes. For example, both groups tended to have poor education outcomes and poor predictors for both ages at leaving care and care placement stability. Also, there was no statistical difference in those who had been looked after at home and those looked after away from home. There was, however, a weak association between career outcomes and difficulties since leaving care, such as offending (p=0.051). For example, almost twice as many young offenders had poor career outcomes when compared to non-offenders in the group (67% and 33% respectively).

Statistically, there was no real indication that aftercare support had any impact upon career outcomes as just over half of young people in both outcomes groups had received intervention throughout the follow-up period. Furthermore, many of the young people who had poor outcomes throughout had been assisted to take part in employment initiatives and basic skills training to help them find a career. It is likely, therefore, that wider social factors will have influenced employment outcomes to some extent. As discussed in Chapter 5, the socio-economic climate within local areas, normative trends in the career trajectories of young people across Scotland and the UK and indeed the difficulties experienced by care leavers (whether emotional, financial or practical) in accessing and sustaining education or a career will impact upon outcomes.

Qualitative analysis of young people's accounts of what had helped them with their career did, however, suggest that support, whether from leaving care teams, other professionals or family and friends could act as a mediating factor to assist some young people to achieve good outcomes despite having poor predictors.

Analysis of those young people who had achieved good outcomes throughout the follow-up period and those who had improved on poor career starting points suggested that a common factor throughout was the availability of either formal or informal support. These young people reported having been assisted by leaving care workers and other professionals, such as careers advisors, the Jobcentre and hostel/homeless unit staff. However, in the absence of these services (and, in some cases, in addition to them), young people had received help from friends and family. As the following illustrations show, there also appeared to be a significant level of motivation to succeed amongst this group.

Brian had been unemployed since leaving care but had attended training courses and a skills for work programme run by the social work department. At T2 he had obtained a college place with the assistance of the programme: 'I only went a couple of times and they got me straight into college...I hope I stick in at college and get a decent job and a house. That's all I want.'

Abby, who had been looked after at home, had failed to get any standard grades and had received no aftercare support since leaving care. She had, however, received help and encouragement (including financial support) from her family to find a training scheme at T2:

> My mum and sisters, they helped me get in to the training services...I have no standard grades and it's much harder to get a job. I'm getting into training because it's not just for the money, it's because I want to be a nursery nurse – get my brain working again and getting an income.

Fiona, a young woman who had been in foster care and who had good educational outcomes, told us at T1 that one of the bad things about her life was 'being unemployed and not having much money'. At T2, having found employment as a care assistant, she said told us:

> I have not received any [leaving care] services. I didn't feel that I needed any. My foster carer has been my main source of support. I also get support from my boyfriend and his family. His mum told me about the job and I completed the application form and made phone calls by myself.

It was apparent that having some form of reliable support was common to most young people with good outcomes as most had good family links or social networks. Those young people without this source of support, however, were able to rely on leaving care staff or social workers. One young man who had been 'deserted' by his family and had been made homeless on several occasions throughout the follow-up period had nevertheless been able to maintain good employment outcomes by managing to continue working despite fairly chaotic and adverse personal circumstances. When asked to sum up any help he had received, Barry told us:

> My social worker gave me money to enable me to continue to work. He's been my social worker for three years. He has said that I can contact him anytime I need to…he's always there for me and can always help me. If he can't give me what I need he'll find an alternative. He's been a brilliant help to me over the past three years – not like the first social worker I had. He also provided me with references for my jobs. The good things are I have money to spend, I have a job. I'm doing a job that I've always wanted to do.

Finding a foothold on the career ladder in the early months after leaving care also appeared to be an important factor in achieving a good career outcome, particularly if, like Barry, young people were assisted to sustain their participation. The majority (70%) of those who had good career starting points were still in employment, education or training at T2 while the majority of those with poor starting points remained unemployed throughout (p=0.002).

In terms of identifying factors that may influence young people's access to different career paths, no clear patterns were discernible for young people who had entered employment or training. There was, however, some evidence that amongst young people looked after away from home those who had successfully continued in education tended to share certain characteristics. Of the three young people (5%) who were in education, two had continued in education throughout the study period and one other young person had successfully completed their education course and found employment. Although the numbers are very small and these findings should be considered indicative rather than conclusive, a brief look at what they had in common gives some indication of the ingredients that may be necessary for educational success.

First, all three young people had been looked after long term in foster placements, the minimum period being six years. Second, two out of the three had a very stable experience of being looked after and the third, although he had made a number of moves over 14 years, managed to settle into a stable foster placement towards the end of his care career. Third, all three had experienced few or no problems at school. They attended regularly, had never been excluded or suspended and two out of three had attained some qualifications at the end of their schooling. Finally, all were continuing their education within the context of a supported environment. Two had been able to remain with their foster carers after formally ceasing to be looked after and the third was living in a semi-independent flat supported by the leaving care team. Furthermore, all were receiving a consistent package of support, including financial assistance to pursue their studies.

Finally, having considered outcomes across a range of life areas (life skills, family and social networks, accommodation and career), we have so far drawn on statistical and qualitative analysis to help us understand what helps young people to make a successful transition from care to post-care living. Further discussion of the issues arising from our analysis of outcomes and intervention is undertaken in the concluding chapter. Before moving on to further analytical interpretations of what helps in leaving care, it is useful to first consider more directly the views of young people who had experienced this transition.

Young people's views: what makes a difference?

In this last section we have presented the views of young people who participated in the study as a means of looking at what makes a difference from the young person's perspective. In particular we have drawn upon responses to the question: 'Based on your own experience, what advice would you give to young people who will be leaving care in the future?' A number of common themes emerged.

Get support

A key message arising from young people's comments was the importance of help and advice. Support, whether from family, friends or professionals, was recognised as being crucial for young people finding their way through the challenges of post-care living.

The importance of having family contact and support were emphasised by Anna: 'Try and get back in contact with your family if you're not in contact with them. Without your family it's hard.' This was echoed in Susan's advice: 'I'd say family is important when you leave care, so try and get back on track with them.'

Friendship was also highlighted in young people's advice to others. Sandra suggested, 'Figure out who your real friends are and forget the rest', while Peter offered advice to others who, like him, may find themselves socially isolated: 'Just keep the head up, it's not easy for people who cannot make pals.' In terms of general support, Penny recommended that young people should 'try and find at least one person you can talk to. If you have one person at least you have something'.

The importance of being able to listen to advice and accept help were also emphasised. Some young people told us that when preparing to leave care it could often be difficult to see the benefit of advice and accept or ask for support. This may be because of the level of input and advice being offered from various sources, or because of young people's desire to be independent and break free from being advised what to do. In Corrine's advice to other young people, she asserted, 'you're your own boss now'. However, reconciling this feeling with the need for ongoing support was an issue for many young people.

In recognising this dilemma, Carrie suggested: 'Listen to advice from professionals and take into consideration what they are saying to you. When I was in care I thought I knew things, but it was only now that I look back and realise I didn't.' Similar advice came from Jessica, whose own experience prompted her to note: 'Even though it feels that all adults are getting at you, they have your best interests at heart. Most of the time they are right although you don't realise it until later.'

While young people were clear that other care leavers should not be afraid to have their say and voice their views and needs – 'take control of your right to speak, rather than being just a little person they're making decisions about' – they urged young people to make the most of the support and advice on offer.

Chloe commented: 'Get as much help as you can off social work and throughcare; do what's asked of you and you might get what you want.' Alan's advice to others was 'basically, to just let the staff help you, they are there for your best interests.'

Stay out of trouble

Another prominent message to come from young people was 'keep out of trouble'. Advice to avoid crime, negative peer pressure and substance misuse often came from their own experience.

Ann, who had experienced problems with offending since leaving care, warned other young people: 'You have to learn that when you get into trouble with the police they are always going to come out on top.'

Josh, meanwhile, cautioned others on the wider problems arising from hanging about with the 'wrong crowd':

What I'd say is try not to get involved. Peer pressure is a big thing...a really big thing. Don't get involved with drink or drugs. You've got plenty of years to go if you want to drink when you're older and stay out of trouble.

Oliver offered a wide range of advice to young people leaving care in the future. Again, much of this was based on his own experiences:

If you run away and stuff, stop doing it. It doesn't achieve anything. Use contraception – you don't want to be a parent, it's hard work. Don't get in with the wrong people and try to save money and get a job.

Get an education
Getting an education also featured in the advice young people offered to others. Many recognised the value of qualifications and training in terms of getting employment, and for some, in generating a sense of achievement. Jessica advised, 'Stick in at school, it's important', and Lyn observed: 'I would say education is the big thing now. It's very important and it will always be something you've achieved in your life.'

Iris, who had truanted and been excluded while at school, commented, 'I'd tell other people – don't skip school. Get to school; I wish I had, it might have got me a decent job.'

The value of education and training after care was also highlighted. Heather told others: 'If you're advised to go to college, force yourself to follow it even if you don't like it because it will pay off in the end.'

Don't leave too soon
One of the most significant pieces of advice from young people to those leaving care in the future was 'don't leave too soon'. A considerable number of young people commented on the importance of being well prepared and having somewhere to go when moving on from care. Many echoed Jim's comment: 'It's not as easy as you think.'

Gill advised, 'Don't leave too soon because it won't be easy. I've been trained how to deal with adult life. Don't believe it's as easy as people tell you. Just be mature about it. Don't run before you can walk.'

The importance of throughcare preparation and aftercare support was evidenced by several young people. Emma, for example, commented, 'Make sure you are on your feet first, make sure you're prepared and plan ahead. Don't leave on your 16th birthday just because you can.'

Liz, meanwhile, told us, 'I would advise anyone leaving care to get in touch with leaving care workers. Don't jump into a flat of your own too soon. You don't realise how hard it's going to be on your own.'

Similar sentiments were expressed by Carol: 'Don't do what I done and leave care as soon as you can without proper help on things like budgeting and housing.' And also from Brian, who advised: 'Don't leave care unless you've got a good job and a house.'

Deb, who had left care two months before her 18th birthday, told us:

> They should try and stay longer. I decided to stay in care a bit longer. I think if you do that you get to appreciate what's going on around you. Sixteen is far too young to let someone out into their own house.

Be positive and make something of your life

Finally, many of the young people who participated in the study were positive about their futures. Iona advised: 'Look forward and not back. Make something with your life.'

When asked what they hoped the future would bring, embarking upon a career path together with having their own home with family and friends around them were common aspirations.

Emma told us, 'I do one day hope to be working. I don't want to have all these qualifications and then waste them', and William said, 'I'd hope to be a joiner or get a roofing job. I want a proper job. I'd like to have a happy life, be married and everything.'

Maggie also planned to make something of her life; she told us: 'I want to get myself a decent job. Go to college and get qualified and get a better job. Get a better house. My house! When I've got enough money, have a family.'

Finally Lewis's hopes to overcome the difficulties of past experiences and lead a 'normal' life encapsulated the hopes of many of the young people who shared their views and experiences with us:

> It's difficult for young people moving out of care and you still carry the memories of the children's home with you. I just want to make something of my life; I want as normal [a life] as any other person. I'd have a job, a family, a car and my own family around if I needed support.

Conclusion

Helping young people such as Lewis, mentioned above, to prevail despite their early difficulties and to realise their aspirations is the central challenge facing throughcare and aftercare services. By drawing on young people's experiences, this chapter has attempted to identify the key factors involved in assisting young people to achieve positive outcomes and those that impede their progress. In doing so, it has offered some direction, or at the very least, confirmed existing knowledge, as to what makes a difference in supporting young people to make successful transitions from substitute care to post-care adult living.

As we have seen, instability in care through placement movement, experiencing educational difficulties and disruption such as truancy, and difficulties associated with substance misuse, offending, and wider emotional and behavioural issues can have a negative impact upon young people's outcomes and general life chances after leaving care, particularly in the absence of support.

Having good preparation and good life skills, achieving good outcomes in accommodation and career in the early months after leaving care and remaining relatively free of difficulties made for greater success in achieving good outcomes and improved progress towards a successful transition to post-care living. This was particularly so where young people also had consistent (or accessible), reliable and effective support, whether from family, friends or professionals. Such support could often mediate against early risk indicators and difficulties experienced during or after care. There was, however, an indication that for many young people support could fall away in the early months after moving on. There was also the danger that those young people who may appear to be more settled than others, or who have remained or returned home to family, may not be entitled to the same level of professional aftercare support as those who appear more chaotic or troubled.

Finally, there was clear evidence from young people's own advice as to what makes a difference in leaving care. Key messages included the importance of: making the most of the support while looked after, whether from carers, support workers or friends and family; getting an education; not leaving care too early (both in terms of age and preparedness); and, with the help of support systems (both formal and informal), working towards overcoming past and present difficulties so as to build a positive and inclusive future.

Notes

1 The terms T1 (short for Time 1) and baseline refer to the first point of data collection from young people and their support workers, and are used interchangeably. T1/baseline took place on average five months after leaving care for the follow-up group. The terms T2 and follow-up stage have also been used interchangeably. They

refer to the second point of data collection which took place six months on from T1, at an average of 11 months after leaving care.

2 The findings presented in this section should be treated with a degree of caution. Information for young people in the follow-up group was gathered at an average of five months after moving on from care at baseline (T1) and 11 months at follow-up. This is a relatively short period in which to reach conclusions as to the effects or results of the care experience and any intervention. Although we have used the term 'final outcomes', they should in fact be seen as indications of the progress being made by young people as they embark upon the transition to independence and adulthood.

3 Cronbach's alpha was 0.902 for the preparation scale and 0.7312 for the coping scale, indicating a good level of reliability between the items.

4 The alpha statistic for each of these sub-scales was 0.828, 0.757, 0.785 and 0.893 respectively.

5 The alpha scores for these two scales were 0.742 and 0.750 respectively.

6 The test result is Kendall's tau-b=0.297, p=0.003.

7 We were unable to assess accommodation coping outcomes for the remaining cases (33%) due to missing information.

Chapter 9

Conclusion: Developing Throughcare and Aftercare Services

Introduction

This book has explored the way local authorities have carried out their duties and powers under the Children (Scotland) Act (1995) to promote throughcare and aftercare services for young people they have looked after. The findings are based upon a national policy survey of all local authorities and a range of other agencies who provide services, as well as an in-depth study of the experiences of young people leaving care in three very different areas of Scotland.

The book tells the story of young people's journeys to adulthood – their experiences of living in care, leaving care and their lives after care – and how they have been helped or hindered by their bureaucratic parent. In this concluding chapter we will discuss the main messages from our study and explore the implications of our findings for the development of throughcare and aftercare services. However, we will begin by outlining the main changes in law and policy that have taken place since the completion of our research, to set our discussion in context.

Legal and policy context

Since we finished our research in 2002 there have been major changes in law and policy introduced by the Scottish Parliament and Executive. They were informed by the recommendations of the Working Group on the Throughcare and Aftercare of Looked After Children in Scotland, whose members were representative of the main interest groups, including social work, housing, careers, young people, the Scottish Throughcare and After-care Forum, Social Inclusion Partnerships (SIPs) and the Scottish Executive. It was set up in 1999 and reported in 2002, drawing on, among other sources, our own research findings.

The Working Group specifically considered the implications of the Children (Leaving Care) Act 2000. This legislated for the transfer of financial support for 16- and 17-year-olds from the Department for Work and Pensions (DWP) to the local authority; a duty to assess and meet the needs of young people in and leaving care; pathway planning; the appointment of personal advisors; assistance with education and training up to the age of 24; maintenance in suitable accommodation and a duty to keep in touch by the 'responsible authority', that is, by the local authority that 'looked after' the young person.

First of all, following the recommendations of the Working Group, the Scottish Executive delayed the implementation of Section 6 of the Children (Leaving Care) Act 2000, concerning the transfer of financial support for qualifying 16- and 17-year-old care leavers to local authorities. This delay, until April 2004, was to allow local authorities time to develop the information systems to identify young people entitled to receive benefits. As our policy survey had shown, half of the local authorities had experienced difficulties in accessing and collating data on the numbers of young people eligible for throughcare and aftercare services.

Second, the Regulations of Care (Scotland) Act 2001 was also implemented from the beginning of April 2004. Section 73(1) of this Act strengthened the provisions of Section 29 of the Children (Scotland) Act 1995 by placing upon local authorities duties to:

- carry out an assessment of the needs of young people who have been looked after who they have a duty or power to advise, guide or assist under Section 29

- establish a procedure for considering representations, including complaints, made to them about the discharge of their functions under Section 29.

Third, Section 73(2) of the above Act gave Scottish Ministers the power to introduce new regulations and, following a consultation process, the *Supporting Young People Leaving Care in Scotland, Regulations and Guidance on Services for Young People Ceasing to be Looked After by Local Authorities* was published. This detailed the new Regulations and Guidance, to be implemented from April 2004, governing the involvement of young people; the categories of young people to be supported; the definition and duties of the responsible local authority; needs assessment and pathway planning; the role of the pathway co-ordinator and young person's supporter; financial assistance; accommodation; complaints; and information gathering and sharing.

Fourth, the Scottish Executive funded the development of *Pathways* by Barnardo's Scotland and the Scottish Throughcare and Aftercare Forum in partnership with young people's focus groups from Barnardo's and Who Cares? Scotland. This is a set of materials planned in conjunction with the new Guidance and Regulations to provide a framework for needs assessment and action planning for young people who have been looked after. Keeping the young person at the centre of the process is the guiding principle: 'Each module looks at a particular area of your life and helps you think about what things are going well, what things you are concerned about and any action that needs to be taken' (Scottish Executive 2004).

It is divided into seven modules: lifestyle, family and friends, health and well-being, learning and work, where I live, money, rights and legal issues. For each module there are three sections: my pathway views, pathway assessment and pathway plan.

Fifth, the Scottish Executive launched a series of measures to increase the educational chances of young people in and leaving public care. As corporate parents, local authorities are responsible for overseeing the educational needs of young people in their care and in January 2002 the Minister for Education, Cathy Jamieson, launched a series of targets and indicators aimed at driving up the educational participation and performance of looked after children. These targets state that:

- all looked after children should receive full-time education

- all looked after children should have a care plan which adequately addresses educational needs

- all schools should have a teacher designated to championing the interests of these children.

One year on, the Minister reported that further work was needed: 'Reports back from councils show progress is being made but there remains a great deal to be done. Access to education is a basic right; too many of those cared for by local authorities are still being let down' (Cathy Jamieson, Education Minister, speaking in Parliament, February 2003). Further strategies to promote education have included making money available for the purchase of books, computer equipment and homework materials for every looked after child in Scotland.

Finally, as regards accommodation, new arrangements for housing support services were introduced at the beginning of April 2003 under the Supporting People Initiative and care leavers will be able to access these services. Also, the Homelessness (Scotland) Act 2003 has amended Section 25 of the Housing (Scotland) Act 1987 to extend 'priority need' to 16- and 17-year-olds and 18- to 20-year-olds who were looked after by a local authority, assessed as homeless.

The impact of these changes has been to both strengthen and widen the scope of the legal framework. Also, through the introduction of *Pathways* there is the potential for a more consistent and structured approach to needs assessment and pathway planning. However, these changes by themselves will not lead to improved outcomes for young people leaving care. Our research – the policy study and interviews, our descriptive survey and outcome analysis – as well as the findings from other studies of care leavers, highlight a number of key areas for the development of more effective throughcare and aftercare services.

Throughcare and aftercare: key areas
Stability, continuity and being settled
Throughcare and aftercare services need to build upon good quality care while young people are looked after. Young people who experience stable placements and are settled at the time of leaving care are more likely to have positive outcomes than those who have experienced further movement and disruption during their time in care and after they leave (Biehal *et al.* 1995; Sinclair *et al.* 2003).

Stability is important in two respects. First of all, it provides the young person with a warm and redeeming relationship with a carer – a compensatory secure attachment, which may in itself reduce the likelihood of placement breakdown (Rutter *et al.* 1998). Second, and not necessarily dependent on the first, stability may provide continuity of care in young people's lives, which may give them security and contribute to positive educational and career outcomes (Jackson 2002; Jackson *et al.* 2003).

Consistent with the findings from earlier research, we found that in our study all the young people who had positive educational outcomes had experienced stability in their last care placement.

Being settled also matters even if young people have experienced earlier instability. We found that young people who were settled in their accommodation, or in education, employment and training at the time of leaving care also had positive career outcomes six months later.

Education and careers
As suggested above, stability and continuity were the foundation stones for educational success in our study. But this only applied to just over a third of our young people – the majority had very poor education outcomes at the time of leaving care and when interviewed six months later. Also, truancy and exclusion were common experiences for three-quarters of the young people we surveyed. We found that disruption to education through truancy

was also associated with offending and substance misuse amongst young people and a predictor of poor accommodation outcomes.

Career outcomes for our young people were also generally poor. At the time of leaving care over half of the young people were unemployed and six months later nearly two-thirds of young people had failed to find stable employment, education or training. Most of these young people were dependent upon benefits. Although our young people were not immune to the wider changes in the youth labour market which impact upon young people generally, our analysis of what made a difference, given young people's starting points, showed that young people who achieved positive outcomes were able to take advantage of formal or informal support or some combination of both.

The importance of young people having a positive experience of school, including achieving educational success, cannot be underestimated in today's society which places such a high premium on academic and vocational qualifications. There is a clear association between educational success and the resilience of young people from both disadvantaged family backgrounds and young people living in care.

Also, enhancing the career chances of care leavers needs to build upon the educational progress while young people are looked after. This is clearly recognised in the Social Exclusion Unit's report, *A Better Education for Children in Care* (SEU 2003). The need for five key changes is spelt out in their report: greater stability, less time out of school, help with schoolwork, more help from home to support schoolwork, and improved health and well-being.

Research studies show that placement stability, positive encouragement from carers, proactive placement, school and education service links, as well as compensatory assistance, can contribute to improved educational outcomes (Biehal *et al.* 1995; SEU 2003). Conversely, teachers' negative attitudes, low carer expectations, bullying and giving little priority to education may all inhibit young people's educational progress (Jackson 1994; Parker *et al.* 1991).

In helping young people improve their career opportunities there is evidence from evaluated practice that young people can be assisted by: assessing their skills and abilities (including any achievements and potential they may have), and providing ongoing support to maintain motivation and to assist those wishing to return to learning, and remain in training or employment (Wade 2003). Also, inter-agency links can provide access to career opportunities and to plan service developments – including links with Careers (Scotland), Connexions, training agencies, further and higher education colleges, employers, benefits agencies and youth services

(Department of Health 1997; SEU 2003; Smith 1994; Wade 2003). A number of local authorities have been successful in developing work experience placements for care leavers through collaborative working and the Who Cares? Trust Employability Programme (Department of Health/Centrepoint 2002).

Age of leaving

Most of our young people (93%) had moved on from care before they were 18 years of age, the average age being just 16. Nearly three-quarters of the young people we surveyed legally left care or moved to independence at 15 (21%) or 16 (52%). Although some young people felt they were ready to move on and benefited from the supported accommodation they moved into, others felt that they were 'being pushed out' or pressurised by staff or carers who thought they were too old for foster care or their children's home. Other young people had to leave time-limited placements.

In comparison to their peers in the general population, many of these young people have to cope with the challenges and responsibilities of major changes in their lives – in leaving foster care or residential care and setting up home, in leaving school and entering the world of work, or being unemployed and surviving on benefits, and entering parenthood – at a far younger age. In short, many have compressed and accelerated transitions to adulthood (Stein 2002). They are denied the psychological opportunity and space to focus, or to deal with issues over time, which is how most young people cope with the challenges of transition (Coleman and Hendry 1999).

Just a few of our young people were able to remain in foster care placements after they were 18 and had legally left care. This was a very successful arrangement in that it provided stability, continuity and the opportunity for a more gradual transition from care. But it was very much the exception.

A major challenge to the development of more effective throughcare and aftercare services is to reflect normative transitions to adulthood. However, research studies completed since the 1980s show that a majority of young people leave care before they are 18, suggesting that it will require a radical shift in culture and attitude amongst policy makers, social workers and carers to bring about such a significant change in the system.

Throughcare: preparation for leaving care

Our study showed that there was a significant link between the throughcare preparation young people received while they were looked after and how well they coped six months after leaving care. Preparing young people in domestic skills: cooking, budgeting and shopping; lifestyle concerns: safe sex, alcohol, drugs and smoking; social skills: hobbies, socialising, boy and girlfriends; and self-care skills: skin and hair care, healthy eating and keeping fit, made a difference to their lives. We found that 'preparation' was significantly related to 'coping' after care. Domestic tasks and lifestyle issues were the most important in terms of overall coping but it was also enhanced by social skills preparation. Young women generally felt better prepared for domestic tasks, reflecting traditional gender-stereotyped roles.

The main implication of our research for the development of throughcare and aftercare service is that more young people should have planned throughcare programmes – less than half of the young people we surveyed received a planned programme. Young people on a home supervision requirement may benefit (see policy discussion below) and young men should be better prepared.

Evaluations of good practice in regard to preparation point to the importance of assessment to identify young people's needs and how they will be met: providing ongoing support and opportunities for participation, involving discussion, negotiation and risk-taking and the gradual learning of skills, in the context of a stable placement (Clayden and Stein 1996).

Also, preparation should attach equal importance to practical, emotional and interpersonal skills and be responsive to gender differences, ethnic diversity and any disability or health needs the young person may have (Rabiee and Priestley 2001). Specialist leaving care schemes can assist carers with the development of skills training programmes, and by offering intensive compensatory help at the aftercare stage (Biehal *et al.* 1995).

Aftercare: formal and informal support

In addition to throughcare preparation, this study set out to evaluate the effectiveness of aftercare arrangements and, more specifically, the contribution made by the different models of leaving care services in our three areas. Although the numbers of participating young people meant that we were not able to make comparisons between the three models, we were able to explore the contribution made by formal and informal support. Our analysis across a range of outcome areas (education, employment and training, accommodation and well-being) showed that the mediating factor between young people's poor starting points and good outcomes, for those young people who achieved them, was often reliable and accessible support, whether provided by formal services or informal family and friendship networks.

Formal support in our study was provided by local authority specialist leaving care teams, children and family social workers who were assisting young people leaving care, foster and residential carers as well as workers from other agencies.

Both our non-specialist children and family teams and our specialist leaving care teams had partnership arrangements with voluntary and statutory agency projects within their areas. In two of our areas, Barnardo's 16+ projects assisted young people with accommodation and a range of personal support needs. In our third area the leaving care team worked with a specialist education, employment and training project. Also, one of our areas belonged to an SIP aimed specifically at improving services for young people leaving care.

As our study has demonstrated, young people were being assisted with their accommodation, their careers, their finances, as well as any other personal support needs that emerged – such as issues related to their health and well-being. We found that the support provided by our specialist leaving care workers was likely to be more frequent and seen by young people as more helpful than that provided by non-specialist social workers. Our young people valued regular personal support, reliability and availability and our specialist services were more able to offer this than social workers. In addition to leaving care teams and social workers, our young people identified a range of other workers who had assisted them after leaving care. This included health professionals, housing support staff and advocacy workers, reflecting the established inter-agency links.

The contribution of formal and informal support is clearly evident in relation to accommodation. Our research showed that although nearly two-thirds of young people had moved three or more times since leaving care and 40 per cent experienced homelessness, most of these young people were supported and assisted out of homelessness and three-quarters achieved 'good' or 'fair' outcomes. Formal housing support was connected to well-developed working relationships and protocols with housing providers.

There is clear evidence in our study that both our specialist leaving care services and social workers were working with young people who had very poor or missing family ties – they were reaching out to the young people who needed them most. Nearly two-thirds of young people leaving residential care were in contact with a leaving care worker (65%) or a social worker (65%) compared to those from foster care (62% and 42% respectively) and those on supervision living at home (12% and 4% respectively) – although for all young people contact tended to decrease over time.

Maintaining contact with former carers has the potential to offer young people both continuity and another source of support although this will depend on the quality of the caring relationships. We found that about half of our young people had some form of contact, from face-to-face to telephone contact, with their ex-foster or residential carers. As with formal support, this also tended to fall away over time.

Young people who had positive family links (i.e. helpful contact) benefited from both practical and emotional support at the time of leaving and during the six-month period after leaving care. In this context, family included extended family members where parental relationships had broken down; brothers and sisters, grandparents, aunts and uncles were all seen as helpful by young people. Strong and positive social networks were also helpful to young people, especially in feeling good about themselves – that is, their sense of self-esteem and well-being. These networks protected them from loneliness and isolation.

The availability of formal and informal support can improve young people's outcomes after they leave care. However, it will need to be based on a very rigorous assessment. We know that in some cases birth family links and peer influences can be highly problematic and hold young people back from being able to move on successfully (Biehal and Wade 1996; Sinclair *et al.* 2003).

At the planning stage, an assessment of young people's sources of support should be based upon family, including extended family, carer links and friendship networks, as well as formal support. This may include arrangements for young people to live close to positive support networks, a continuing role for carers to support young people and the option for young people to remain with carers on a supported lodging basis (Dixon and Stein 2002; Fry 1992; Wade 1997). There is also evidence that specialist leaving care schemes can play an important role in helping young people form new networks and relationships (Biehal *et al.* 1995).

Policy framework

In addition to the issues discussed above arising from the findings of our descriptive survey and outcomes analysis, our policy survey also identified how the policy framework for the development of throughcare and aftercare services can be improved.

First, throughcare and aftercare services need to operate within a comprehensive policy framework. This should include a clear definition of services in Children's Services Plans, detailed and transparent policy and procedures and guidance on throughcare and aftercare services for all relevant parties, including foster carers, parents and young people. Also, although most of the authorities we surveyed had a lead officer, this was not always at the appropriate level to represent throughcare and aftercare services within the department, the wider authority and external agencies.

Second, our survey showed that where corporate and inter-agency working arrangements existed they were seen as generally positive and they increased young people's access to a wide range of resources, including accommodation, employment and training. However, our survey also indicated that better communications, clearer procedures and formal agreements could be extended, especially to education, employment and training, health and children's reporters. Of particular concern was the low priority given to health and well-being, although this was acknowledged by the local authorities we surveyed.

Third, as discussed above, throughcare programmes can greatly assist young people after they leave care. Our policy survey adds to this picture. It showed that most young people on supervision living at home were less likely to receive throughcare than other eligible young people living in children's homes and foster care. However, these young people may be living in very difficult family situations that will not provide them with such preparation, especially if they have to move on. Our survey also showed that local authorities should ensure that they cover all the main elements of preparation (self-care, practical skills, interpersonal skills, education and identity) as well as considering the specific needs of different groups of young people. It may well be that the introduction of *Pathways* will address these concerns.

Fourth, and again as discussed above, informal and formal support made a positive difference to many of our young people's lives. Our policy survey highlights the need for more to be done to promote the continuity of care, by giving more policy recognition to building on positive formal and informal networks of support. Also, our survey showed there was little attention paid to the process of ending personal support. Should there be more formal procedures for a review and exit interview?

Fifth, most of the local authorities we surveyed acknowledged difficulties in collating data on young people's eligibility as well as collecting statistical monitoring information and outcome data for throughcare and aftercare services. Half of our authorities were unable to identify as a matter of course all young people who were eligible to receive services and very few had effective monitoring and evaluation systems in place. Most local authorities needed to develop the electronic information systems necessary to the effective costing and planning of services.

Finally, it is important that young people are able to participate in the development of services and that they are given the opportunity to have their views heard. Most of the local authorities were committed to involving young people in the process of formulating and reviewing policy and practice. The former included their involvement in the development of policy, procedures and guidance. The latter included their involvement in the care planning and review process. There were also several examples of wider consultation exercises with young people via questionnaires and focus groups. Of course, listening to young people was central to our own research. Our experience demonstrates that it is only by seeking young people's views and hearing their stories of care and moving on that we can learn more about what helps them manage the process of leaving care.

Concluding comment

Leaving care has become an increasing priority on the political agenda. The legislative and policy developments which have taken place in recent years and which are continuing to be implemented are beginning to change the shape and focus of services for those in and leaving care.

Our study focused on one of the more central legislative developments in Scotland – throughcare and aftercare services for young people leaving care under the Children (Scotland) Act 1995. It explored the experience of leaving care from the perspective of young people (service users), workers (front-line service providers) and policy staff (service developers).

Our research has shown that young people leaving care are a diverse group. It has also shown that they are a vulnerable group. This is recognised in recent changes to both strengthen and widen the scope of the legal and policy framework to provide assistance to young people in and leaving care across Scotland and the UK. However, major challenges still remain to improve their life chances: providing them with greater stability and continuity while they are looked after; increasing the help available to assist them with their education and careers; giving them the opportunity for a more gradual transition from care more akin to other young people's journeys to adulthood today; ensuring better all-round preparation for leaving care; and providing more consistent and ongoing support after they leave care. In working towards meeting these challenges, throughcare and aftercare services can and do make a real difference to the lives of some of Scotland's most vulnerable young people.

Appendix: Methodology

The study

The research study on which this book is based was carried out between 1999 and 2001. Its primary focus was on support for young people leaving care, under the Children (Scotland) Act 1995. A number of key questions underpinned the research. For instance, we were interested in finding out how local authorities were meeting their responsibilities under the Act in delivering throughcare and aftercare services to young people leaving care. More crucially, perhaps, how were these arrangements working on the ground or in other words how effective were their arrangements for preparing young people for and supporting them through the transition from care to independent adult living?

In addressing these key questions the research was able to:

- describe throughcare and aftercare arrangements across all local authorities in Scotland

- examine the extent to which the principles and guidance enshrined in the 1995 Act were reflected in current local authority practice

- explore in detail throughcare and aftercare policy and practice in three local authorities

- describe the leaving care experience and assess early post-care outcomes for young people moving on from care, based on the experiences of young people themselves and the perceptions of their leaving care support workers.

In short, the study provided an exploration of how support for young people leaving care works in practice within the wider policy context of throughcare and aftercare under the Children (Scotland) Act 1995.

Design of the study

The study comprised two stages. The first stage involved a national policy survey of Scottish local authorities and other relevant service providers. From this information we were able to explore the different arrangements employed by distinctive models of service delivery in order to put together a picture of throughcare and aftercare services in Scotland.

The second stage involved conducting detailed case studies of three local authorities, selected to be representative of the main models of leaving care services and the geographic diversity of Scotland. The aim of this stage was to reflect upon the ways in which throughcare and aftercare arrangements were working in practice. Information was gathered from young people and their main support worker.

In addition, telephone interviews were carried out with key informants drawn from senior management to reflect upon and update policy developments in the three study areas.

Data collection

Data was collected via postal questionnaires, face-to-face interviews, telephone interviews and reviews of policy and practice documents. Methods varied according to the type and source of the data and were adapted to meet the needs of the respondent and to facilitate maximum response rates. For example, in cases where young people were unwilling to be interviewed, a postal questionnaire was used. Also, where workers failed to complete a postal questionnaire, telephone interviews were often adopted to collect necessary data.

Stage one: the national policy survey

The Children (Scotland) Act 1995 places responsibility on local authorities to provide throughcare and aftercare services for looked after young people and care leavers. The Act envisages that these services will be provided by the social work department in collaboration with other statutory and voluntary agencies. It was therefore important that we obtained information from the perspective of the social work department together with other agencies that may be involved in providing services to young people who are preparing to leave or who have left care.

A policy questionnaire was distributed to all 32 Scottish social work departments during March 2000. Information was sought on the range of services provided to care leavers, inter-agency planning and working and procedures for monitoring and evaluating the service. Details on the number of service users and the size and structure of the team were also collected along with supporting documentation on local policy and practice procedures. Reminder letters and telephone calls assisted a final response rate of 97 per cent (n=31), with only one local authority questionnaire outstanding.

Supplementary questionnaires focusing on the working arrangements between the social work department and other agencies were sent to a range of statutory service providers, voluntary agencies and projects working with young people. This included local authority housing and education departments, employment services, the Scottish Children's Reporters Administration[1] and a range of 'other' agencies, such as health boards, primary care trusts, other housing providers and a range of specialist and voluntary projects offering support to young people. In all, a total of 178 supplementary questionnaires were sent out, and 99 (56%) were returned.[2]

Stage two: the local authority case studies
RESEARCH AREAS
From the results of the policy survey three local authority areas were selected for participation in stage two of the research. These were County, City and Shire (see Chapter 2 for a description of the areas).

The second stage began in July 2000 and involved contacting young people from across the three local authorities. Young people were eligible to take part in the study if:

- they were between 15½ and 19 years of age
- they had been legally discharged from care or had moved onto independent living between June 2000 and January 2001.

This included:

- young people whose home supervision requirement had been discharged (whether they remained at home or not)
- young people who had legally left care (whether they returned home, moved to independent living or remained with foster carers)
- young people who had moved to independent living whether they were still on a care order or not (i.e. looked after and previously looked after).

This stage involved a baseline study and a six-month follow-up study. Young people were therefore contacted at two points in time: Time 1 (T1), which involved a questionnaire being administered to young people soon after they left care, and Time 2 (T2), which involved an interview or questionnaire six months later.

At T1 and T2, a questionnaire was sent to the social worker or specialist leaving care worker who had responsibility for the young person. This allowed us to gather corresponding information from a professional perspective.

RESEARCH INSTRUMENTS
The T1 questionnaires included a brief exploration of the young person's care experience, any throughcare support received, their current circumstances, contact with a social worker or leaving care worker and their hopes for the future.

Structured interview schedules for young people at T2 were constructed to gather detailed qualitative information about their present circumstances and any help or support they had received during the intervening months between T1 and T2 (follow-up period).

PARTICIPATION RATES
Of the 212 young people who were identified as eligible and referred to the study by the leaving care teams, around half (n=107) agreed to participate and went on to complete a T1 questionnaire.

A sub-sample of these young people (n=79) were contacted again six months later and asked to participate in a follow-up interview. In addition to having some difficulty in tracing a small proportion (7%) of the sub-sample, 16 per cent felt unable or unwilling to take part. However, 77 per cent (n=61) did go on to complete an interview (n=43) or postal questionnaire (n=18) at the follow-up stage.

Postal questionnaires were sent to workers who held responsibility for each young person who participated in the study at both points in time. Information was received from 77 per cent of workers contacted at T1 and 58 per cent of those contacted at the T2 follow-up stage.[3]

Findings are based on:

Social work department questionnaires	97% of those contacted (n=31)
Supplementary questionnaires	56% of those contacted (n=99)
T1 Young persons' data	51% of those referred (n=107)
T1 Workers' data	77% of those contacted (n=61)
T2 Young persons' data	77% of those contacted (n=61)
T2 Workers' data	58% of those contacted (n=24)

Analysis

Quantitative data

Our main approach to analysing the data was quantitative and involved the use of statistical tests. The statistical package for the social sciences (SPSS) was utilised for this purpose. As a general rule of thumb for statistical analysis, the larger the sample size the better. Given the nature and limitations of our data we opted to use non-parametric statistical tests. These make fewer assumptions about the data and are commonly utilised in social science research. To adjust for the small sample size, SPSS Exact Tests were also used.

REPORTING STATISTICS

For ease of reading we have tried to keep our reporting of statistical tests to a minimum throughout the text. In most cases we will simply give the p-value if a test was statistically significant. A result, $p=0.05$ or less was considered statistically significant for our data. This may be reported as $p=$ followed by the value. Occasionally we have reported the test as $p<$ which simply means p is less than.[4]

Test results and p-values have been reported as a way of supporting our findings. For those readers who prefer to do so, however, it is possible to ignore references to the statistical results throughout the book without losing any of the key information or meaning of the text.

Qualitative data

Qualitative data was explored using a standard database, which enabled us to identify common themes and explore issues within cases and across cases. Factual and descriptive information gathered during the course of interviews and questionnaires was analysed in this way to provide an overall account of the processes and experiences of leaving care from the perspective of young people and their workers.

Ethical considerations

Finally, a discussion of how the study was conducted would not be complete without reference to the ethical framework in which it was implemented. A number of ethical issues arise with regard to the involvement of young people and practitioners in research. Care was taken during all aspects of our research (design, data collection, analysis and reporting) to conduct and report the study according to sound ethical standards.

All research participants were 'volunteers' and were informed as to the study's aims, objectives and importance. The research relationship between participants and the study was also made clear. Researchers involved in fieldwork had experience of interviewing and/or working with young people and had current police checks.

Confidentiality was key and a number of strategies were put in place to ensure it remained so. For example, identifying characteristics were removed from documentation that might be seen by agencies and individuals outside of the research team, and participants in the research were allocated pseudonyms. Data storage was also subject to thorough security procedures.

Notes

1 The Scottish Children's Reporters Administration (SCRA) was established in 1996 under the Local Government etc. (Scotland) Act 1994. The SCRA's remit is to manage and facilitate the performance of the reporters' service under the direction of the Principal Reporter. Children's reporters are part of Scotland's Children's Hearings System. The system deals with children under 16 who are in need, regardless of whether they have committed an offence or have suffered from abuse or neglect. Reporters are full-time officials through whom all referrals must be made. A hearing is composed of three panel members who make the final decision on the appropriate needs of the child and measures of care required.

2 We were unable to gain access to benefits agencies.

3 T2 worker questionnaires were only sent to workers who still had contact with the young person for whom we were seeking information. Twenty young people no longer had contact with a worker at T2, hence information was not collected. So, while 58 per cent of those workers contacted at T2 responded to the questionnaire, this only represented information for 39 per cent or 24 out of the 61 young people

who took part at T2. Information from support workers used throughout therefore refers to up to 77 per cent of the sample at T1 and 58 per cent of the sample at T2.

4   By way of a brief explanation, a p-value gives the probability that a test result can be relied upon to be true, that is to say that it did not occur by chance. P=0.05 simply means that the probability of the result happening by chance is 5 in 100. P<0.01 means that the probability of a result happening by chance is less than 1 in 100 and so on. We have adopted the principle that a test result with a p-value of 0.05 or less is significant. That is to say that the result is unlikely to have happened by chance and is therefore likely to be true of the wider population.

References

BBC News Scotland (2001) 'School system "fails" children in care.' 5 March. http://news.bbc.co.uk/1/ni/scotland/1202055.stm

Barnardo's (2001) *Better Education, Better Futures.* London: Barnardo's.

Biehal, N., Clayden, J., Stein, M. and Wade, J. (1992) *Prepared for Living? A Survey of Young People Leaving the Care of Three Local Authorities.* London: National Children's Bureau.

Biehal, N., Clayden, J., Stein, M. and Wade, J. (1995) *Moving On: Young People and Leaving Care Schemes.* London: HMSO.

Biehal, N. and Wade, J. (1996) 'Looking back, looking forward: care leavers, families and change.' *Children and Youth Services Review 18*, 4/5, 425–445.

Broad, B. (1998) *Young People Leaving Care: Life After the Children Act 1989.* London: Jessica Kingsley Publishers.

Broad, B. (1999) 'Young people leaving care: moving towards "joined up" solutions?' *Children and Society 13*, 2, 81–93.

Broad, B. (2003) *After the Act: Implementing the Children (Leaving Care) Act 2000.* Leicester: Action on Aftercare Consortium and De Montfort University.

Broad, B. (2005) *Improving the Health and Well-being of Young People Leaving Care.* Lyme Regis: RHP

Buchanan, A. (1999) 'Are care leavers significantly dissatisfied and depressed in adult life?' *Adoption and Fostering 23*, 4, 35–40.

Bynner, J. and Parsons, S. (2002) 'Social exclusion and the transition from school to work: the case of young people not in education, employment or training.' *Journal of Vocational Behavior 60*, 289–309.

Cheung, Y. and Heath, A. (1994) 'After care: the education and occupation of adults who have been in care.' *Oxford Review of Education 20*, 3, 361–374.

Clayden, J. and Stein, M. (1996) 'Self-care skills and becoming an adult.' In S. Jackson and S. Kilroe (eds) *Looking After Children, Good Parenting, Good Outcomes, Reader.* London: HMSO.

Coleman, J., Hofler, T. and Kilgore, S. (1981) *Public and Private Schools.* Chicago: National Opinion Research Centre.

Coleman, J.C. and Hendry, L. (1999) *The Nature of Adolescence.* London: Routledge.

Corlyon, J. and McGuire, C. (1997) *Young Parents in Public Care.* London: National Children's Bureau.

Department of Health (1995) *Looking After Children: Good Parenting – Good Outcomes.* London: Department of Health.

Department of Health (1997) *When Leaving Home is also Leaving Care: An Inspection of Services for Young People Leaving Care.* London: Social Services Inspectorate.

Department of Health (1998) *Caring for Children Away from Home: Messages from Research.* Chichester: Wiley.

Department of Health/Centrepoint (2002) *Care Leaving Strategies: A Good Practice Handbook.* London: Department of Health.

Dixon, J. and Stein, M. (2002a) *Still a Bairn: Throughcare and Aftercare Services in Scotland.* Final Report to the Scottish Executive. Edinburgh: Scottish Executive.

Dixon, J. and Stein, M. (2002b) *A Study of Throughcare and Aftercare Services in Scotland.* Scotland's Children, Children (Scotland) Act 1995, Research Findings No. 3. Edinburgh: Scottish Executive.

Emond, R. (2000) 'I Thought it would be a Bed of Roses.' An Exploration into the Difference between the Perception and Reality of Leaving Residential Care. Strathclyde: The Centre for Residential Child Care in Association with The Scottish Throughcare and Aftercare Forum.

Frost, N., Stein, M. and Mills, S. (1999) Understanding Residential Child Care. Aldershot: Ashgate.

First Key (1996) Standards In Leaving Care. Leeds: First Key.

Fry, E. (1992) After Care: Making the Most of Foster Care. London: National Foster Care Association.

Furlong, A., Cartmel. F., Biggart, A., Sweeting, H. and West, P. (2003) Youth Transitions: Patterns of Vulnerability and Processes of Social Inclusion. Edinburgh: Scottish Executive.

Garnett, L. (1992) Leaving Care and After. London: National Children's Bureau.

Gordon, D., Parker, R. Loughran, F. (2000) Disabled Children in Britain: a reanalysis of the OPCS Disability Survey. London: Stationery Office.

HM Inspectors of Schools and the Social Work Services Inspectorate (2001) Learning with Care. The Education of Children Looked After Away from Home by Local Authorities. Edinburgh: Scottish Executive.

House of Commons (1997) Children (Scotland) Act 1995, Chapter 36. London: HMSO.

Jackson, S. (1994) 'Educating children in residential and foster care.' Oxford Review of Education 20, 3, 267–279.

Jackson, S. (ed) (2001) Nobody Ever Told Us School Mattered; Raising the Educational Attainment of Children in Care. London: BAAF.

Jackson, S. (2002) 'Promoting stability and continuity of care away from home.' In D. McNeish, T. Newman and H. Roberts (eds) What Works for Children? Buckingham: Open University Press.

Jackson, S., Ajayi, S. and Quigley, M. (2003) By Degrees: the First Year, from Care to University. London: The Frank Buttle Trust.

Jones, G. (1987) 'Leaving the parental home: an analysis of early housing careers.' Journal of Social Policy 16, 1, 49–74.

Knapp, M. (1989) Measuring Child Care Outcomes. PSSRU Discussion Paper 630. Canterbury: University of Kent.

Koprowska, J. and Stein, M. (2000) 'The mental health of "looked after" young people.' In P. Aggleton, J. Hurry and I. Warwick (eds) Young People and Mental Health. Chichester: Wiley.

MacAskill, S., Cooke, E., Eadie, D. and Hastings, G. (2001) Perceptions of Factors that Promote and Protect against the Misuse of Alcohol amongst Young People and Young Adults. Strathclyde: University of Strathclyde.

Marsh, P. and Peel, M. (1999) Leaving Care in Partnership: Family Involvement with Care Leavers. London: HMSO.

McCann, J.B., James. A., Wilson, S. and Dunn, G. (1996) 'Prevalence of psychiatric disorders in young people in the care system.' British Medical Journal 3313, 1529–1530.

McKeganey, N. and Norrie, J. (1999) 'Pre-teen drug misuse in Scotland.' Addiction Research 7, 6, 493–507.

McLeod, A. (2001) 'Changing patterns of teenage pregnancy: population based study of small areas.' British Medical Journal 232, 199–203.

Meltzer, H., Singelton, N., Lee, A., Bebbington, P., Brugha, T. and Jenkins, R. (2002) The Social and Economic Circumstances of Adults with Mental Disorders. London: HMSO.

Meltzer, H., Garward, R., Corbin, T., Goodman, R. and Ford, T. (2003) The Mental Health of Young People Looked After by Local Authorities in England. London: National Statistics.

Morgan-Klein, B. (1985) Where am I Going to Stay? Edinburgh: Scottish Council for Single Homeless.

National Centre for Social Research (2000) Smoking, Drinking and Drug Misuse Among Young People in 2000. Edinburgh: Scottish Executive.

NHS Scotland (2000) Scottish Health Statistics 2000. Edinburgh: Information and Statistics Division.

Parker, R., Ward, H., Jackson, S., Aldgate, J. and Wedge, P. (1991) *Assessing Outcomes in Childcare.* London: HMSO.

Pinkerton, J. and McCrea, R. (1999) *Meeting the Challenge? Young People Leaving Care in Northern Ireland.* Aldershot: Ashgate.

Rabiee, P. and Priestley, M. (2001) *Whatever Next? Young Disabled People Leaving Care.* Leeds: First Key.

Randall, G. (1988) *No Way Home.* London: Centrepoint.

Randall, G. (1989) *Homeless and Hungry.* London: Centrepoint.

Robson, P., Auckland, K., Crawford, H. and Nevison, C. (1999) *Care Sick? The Physical and Mental Health Needs of a Sample of Young People in Local Authority Residential Care.* Edinburgh: Young Peoples Unit, Royal Edinburgh Hospital.

Rutter, M., Giller, H. and Hagell, A. (1998) *Antisocial Behaviour by Young People.* Cambridge: Cambridge University Press.

Scottish Executive (1999) *Social Justice...A Scotland Where Everyone Matters.* Edinburgh: Social Inclusion Division, Scottish Executive.

Scottish Executive (2000a) *Statistical Bulletin: Housing Series HSG/2000/5, Operation of the Homeless Persons Legislation in Scotland 1988–89 to 1998–99. National and Local Authority Analyses.* Edinburgh: Scottish Executive.

Scottish Executive (2000b) *School Attainment In Scotland: 1992–93 to 1998–99.* National Statistics.

Scottish Executive (2000c) *Social Justice...A Scotland Where Everyone Matters: Annual Report 2000.* Edinburgh: Edinburgh Scottish Executive.

Scottish Executive (2001) *Children Looked After in the Year to 31 March 2000.* Edinburgh: National Statistics.

Scottish Executive (2002) *Children Looked After in the Year to 31 March 2001.* Edinburgh: National Statistics.

Scottish Executive (2003) *Children's Social Work Statistics 2002–2003.* Edinburgh: National Statistics.

Scottish Executive (2004) *Pathways.* Edinburgh: Scottish Executive.

Scottish Executive Central Research Unit (2000) *The 2000 Scottish Crime Survey: First Results.* Crime and Criminal Justice Research Findings No. 51. Edinburgh: Scottish Executive.

Scottish Health Feedback Survey (2001/2002) *Researching the Health of Young People In and Leaving Care in Glasgow. Executive Summary.* Glasgow: The Big Step.

Scottish Office (1997) *Scotland's Children. The Children (Scotland) Act 1995 Regulations and Guidance. Volume 2 Children Looked After by Local Authorities.* Edinburgh: HMSO.

Sinclair, I., Gibbs, I., Baker, C. and Wilson, K. (2003) *What Happens to Foster Children?* Report to the Department of Health. York: University of York.

Smith, C. (ed) (1994) *Partnership in Action: Developing Effective Aftercare Projects.* Westerham: Royal Philanthropic Society.

Social Exclusion Unit (1999) *Teenage Pregnancy.* London: HMSO.

Social Exclusion Unit (2003) *A Better Education for Children in Care.* London: HMSO.

Stein, M. (1990) *Living Out of Care.* Barkingside: Barnardo's.

Stein, M. (1994) 'Leaving care, education and career trajectories.' *Oxford Review of Education 20,* 3, 349–360.

Stein, M. (1997) *What Works in Leaving Care?* Barkingside: Barnardo's.

Stein, M. (2002) 'Leaving care.' In D. McNeish, T. Newman and H. Roberts (eds) *What Works for Children?* Milton Keynes: Open University Press.

Stein, M. and Carey, K. (1986) *Leaving Care.* Oxford: Blackwell.

Stein, M., Pinkerton, J. and Kelleher, P. (2000) 'Young people leaving care in England, Northern Ireland, and Ireland.' *European Journal of Social Work 3,* 3, 235–246.

Stein, M. and Wade, J. (2000) *Helping Care Leavers: Problems and Strategic Responses.* London: Department of Health.

Stein, M. (2004) *What Works for Young People Leaving Care?* Barkingside: Barnardo's.

Tomlinson, J. (1996) *Inclusive Learning. Report of the Learning Difficulties and/or Disabilities Committee.* London: HMSO.

Triseliotis, J., Borland, M., Hill, M. and Lambert, L. (1995) *Teenagers and Social Work Services.* London: HMSO.

Wade, J. (1997) 'Developing leaving care services: tapping the potential of foster carers.' *Adoption and Fostering 21*, 3, 40–49.

Wade, J. (2003) *Leaving Care.* Quality Protects Research Briefing.

Ward, J., Henderson, Z. and Pearson, G. (2003) *One Problem Among Many: Drug Use Among Care Leavers in Transition to Independent Living.* Home Office Research Study 260. London: Home Office.

Subject Index

Page references in *italic* refer to tables and figures.

Author Index